The QIAT Companion

A JUST-IN-TIME RESOURCE FOR IMPLEMENTING THE QUALITY INDICATORS FOR ASSISTIVE TECHNOLOGY

THE QIAT LEADERSHIP TEAM

Gayl Bowser | Diana Foster Carl | Kelly S. Fonner | Terry Vernon Foss
Jane Edgar Korsten | Kathleen M. Lalk | Joan Breslin Larson | Scott Marfilius
Susan R. McCloskey | Penny R. Reed | Joy Smiley Zabala

Copyright © 2020 CAST Inc. and the QIAT Leadership Team

The QIAT Leadership Team: Gayl Bowser, Diana Foster Carl, Kelly S. Fonner, Terry Vernon Foss, Jane Edgar Korsten, Kathleen M. Lalk, Joan Breslin Larson, Scott Marfilius, Susan R. McCloskey, Penny R. Reed, Joy Smiley Zabala

Paperback ISBN 978-1-930583-48-1
Ebook ISBN 978-1-930583-49-8

Library of Congress Control Number: 2019955665

Published by

CAST Professional Publishing
an imprint of CAST, Inc.
Wakefield, MA 01880
www.cast.org

Cover and interior design by Happenstance Type-O-Rama.

Contents

- **Introduction** vii

- **Chapter 1: Quality Indicators for Consideration of Assistive Technology** 1
  - Ensuring Quality in Assistive Technology Consideration 2
  - The Consideration Process 3
  - Next Steps 5
  - Resources 5
  - QIAT Planning Document: Consideration of the Need for AT 7

- **Chapter 2: Quality Indicators for Assessment of Assistive Technology Needs** 9
  - Ensuring Quality Assistive Technology Assessment Services 10
  - The Assessment Process 10
  - Seeking Outside Assistance 13
  - Next Steps 14
  - Resources 14
  - Assistive Technology Assessment Process Planner 16

- **Chapter 3: Quality Indicators for Including Assistive Technology in the IEP** 19
  - Ensuring Quality When Including Assistive Technology in the IEP . . . 20
  - Including AT in the IEP Process 20
  - Next Steps 25
  - Resources 25
  - Assistive Technology in the IEP Planner 27

- **Chapter 4: Quality Indicators for the Implementation of Assistive Technology** 29
  - Ensuring Quality Assistive Technology Implementation Services 30
  - The Implementation Process 30
  - Executing the Plan 33
  - Next Steps 33
  - Resources 34
  - Implementation of Assistive Technology Planner 36

Chapter 5: Quality Indicators for Evaluation of Effectiveness of Assistive Technology 37

Ensuring Quality When Evaluating the Effectiveness of
 Assistive Technology 38
The Planning Process for Evaluating the Effectiveness of
 Assistive Technology 39
Next Steps 42
Resources 43
Plan for Evaluation of Effectiveness of AT Use 44

Chapter 6: Quality Indicators for Assistive Technology Transition . 47

Ensuring Quality in Assistive Technology Transition 48
The AT Transition Planning Process 48
Next Steps 51
Resources 52
Transition Planning Worksheet for AT Users 53

Chapter 7: Quality Indicators for Administrative Support of Assistive Technology Services 57

Ensuring Quality AT Services 58
Building the AT Competence of Educators, Students, and Families 59
Including AT in Program Management 60
Next Steps 61
Resources 61
Administrators' Planner for Effective Technology Supervision
 and Leadership 63
Encouraging Effective Technology Use in Schools 64

Chapter 8: Quality Indicators for Professional Development and Training in Assistive Technology 67

Ensuring Quality Professional Development in Assistive Technology 68
Professional Development Planning Process 68
Evaluating AT Professional Development 70
Next Steps 71
Resources 71
Assistive Technology Professional Development and Training Planner . . . 73

Appendix A: Quality Indicators for Assistive Technology Services, Intent Statements, and Common Errors 75

Quality Indicators for Consideration of Assistive Technology Needs 76
Consideration Quality Indicators 76
Quality Indicators for Assessment of Assistive Technology Needs 78
Quality Indicators for Including Assistive Technology in the IEP 80

Quality Indicators for Assistive Technology Implementation 81
Quality Indicators for Evaluation of the Effectiveness of
   Assistive Technology 83
Quality Indicators for Assistive Technology in Transition 85
Quality Indicators for Administrative Support of Assistive
   Technology Services 86
Quality Indicators for Professional Development and Training in Assistive
   Technology 88

Appendix B: Self-Evaluation Matrices for the Quality Indicators in Assistive Technology Services 91

Introduction to the QIAT Self-Evaluation Matrices 92
References for QIAT Matrices 93
Quality Indicators for Consideration of Assistive Technology Needs 94
Quality Indicators for Assessment of Assistive Technology Needs 96
Quality Indicators for Including Assistive Technology in the IEP 98
Quality Indicators for Assistive Technology Implementation 100
Quality Indicators for Evaluation of the Effectiveness of
   Assistive Technology 102
Quality Indicators for Assistive Technology in Transition 104
Quality Indicators for Administrative Support of Assistive Technology . . .106
Quality Indicators for Professional Development and Training in
   Assistive Technology 108

Appendix C: Self-Evaluation Matrices Summary Sheets 111

QIAT Matrix Worksheet for Consideration of AT Needs 112
QIAT Matrix Worksheet for Assessment of AT Needs 113
QIAT Matrix Worksheet for Including AT in the IEP 114
QIAT Matrix Worksheet for AT Implementation 115
QIAT Matrix Worksheet for Evaluation of Effectiveness of AT 116
QIAT Matrix Worksheet for Assistive Technology Transition 117
QIAT Matrix Worksheet for Administrative Support of AT Services 118
QIAT Matrix Worksheet for Professional Development and Training in AT . . 119

Appendix D: Legal References Related to Assistive Technology . . . 121

Individuals with Disabilities Education Improvement Act of 2004
   (IDEA 2004) 121
Legislative Branch Appropriations Act, Public Law 104-197 129
Assistive Technology Act of 1998, Public Law 105-394 131

About the Authors 133

Introduction

People at all levels of the education system—from U.S. Department of Education to classrooms across the country—are committed to helping students, families, professionals (e.g., teachers, therapists, principals, superintendents), and communities work together to meet the educational needs of every student. This includes making sure every student, including those with disabilities, have what they need to participate in and benefit from learning opportunities.

The content of the *QIAT Companion* is based on practical suggestions for implementing information contained in the book, *Quality Indicators for Assistive Technology: A Comprehensive Guide to Assistive Technology Services* (2015). The book, which was developed by a team of experienced leaders in the field of assistive technology (AT) in education, reflects work and ideas that unfolded over nearly two decades. It includes contributions and feedback from thousands of educators and families. It also provides extensive support for the development and implementation of AT services, including research-based information, resources, and scenarios. These collectively support AT decision-making and actions at all points of AT service delivery and ensures that they

- align with specific areas of special education processes;
- describe the core components of quality AT services in eight areas; and
- require a team approach that emphasizes student and family voice.

The indicators, intent statements, and supporting materials for each area are used as guideposts for developing and sustaining effective, efficient, and ethical AT services across the country and internationally. The QIAT Companion distills the information presented in *Quality Indicators for Assistive Technology: A Comprehensive Guide to Assistive Technology Services* in order to provide educators and families with an efficient, action-based resource.

Assistive Technology Guiding Principles

Although state education agencies and local school districts have long been committed to providing the individualized supports that enable students with disabilities to be actively engaged in learning, many educators and families may be unfamiliar with AT and related topics. The following guiding principles contribute to a foundational understanding of AT and its role in supporting students:

- **The purpose of AT is to enhance a student's capabilities and lower barriers to participation and achievement in customary environments.**

    Understanding what participation and achievement "look like" in the student's customary environments and identifying the barriers the student experiences when facing tasks in those environments is critical to meaningful decision-making about the AT devices and services the student requires.

- **The provision of AT devices and services is a legal requirement.**

    Public schools must, by law, ensure that AT devices and services are made available to students who need them to receive a free appropriate public education (FAPE). AT devices and services may be a part of a student's special education, related services, or supplementary aids and services. (For more detailed information, see Appendix D, "Legal References Related to Assistive Technology.")

- **Individualized Education Program (IEP) teams are responsible for making decisions about AT devices and services.**

    IEP teams are charged with considering whether AT devices and services are needed and, if they are, with determining what is needed. IEP teams also must decide whether a student needs AT devices at home, in the community, or in other settings.

- **Any item can be AT if it is needed to increase, maintain, or improve the functional capabilities of a student with disabilities.**

    Such items can range from "low tech," like pencil grips, to "high tech" computerized or electronic devices. How we define AT depends on the learner's needs and how the item is used. For example, if a software program available to all students includes an option for reading information aloud, using that feature is a choice for most students. For students for whom the read-aloud feature is a choice, it is not AT. However, if an individual student is unable to see or decode text fluently and *requires* the read-aloud feature in the program to have access to the content, it is AT for that student.

- **AT services can include any service that assists a student with the selection, acquisition, and use of an AT device.**

    Providing AT devices without the necessary AT services often fails to lead to expected outcomes. If no services are provided, AT may become yet another barrier to achievement. The range of services may include evaluation, coordination of services, training, and customizing the AT. Think of AT services like all the services related to buying a car. Providing the vehicle is only one step. The driver may need driving lessons, and the vehicle itself will certainly need regular evaluation and maintenance. Maps or a GPS will be helpful as the driver sets out toward a destination. AT services are just as crucial to students using AT devices as automotive services are to drivers. They ensure that students can use their AT to get where they need to go in a timely manner with as little frustration as possible.

- **A collaborative team approach is required.**

  Effective, efficient AT efforts at all stages of implementation involve ongoing work by teams that include educators, students, their families, and others, as appropriate. Individual team members bring unique perspectives and contributions to the team. All may not be—and do not have to be—up to date on all of the latest devices, hardware, and software. Some will have experience with and knowledge of the student, others will bring experience and knowledge of the student's customary environments and the tasks that are a part of active participation and learning. Together they can describe the student, the environments, and the tasks, and when needed, seek assistance with tools that can help the student do the tasks that need to be done when and where they occur.

- **AT is related to function, not to a disability category.**

  Effective selection of AT devices requires an understanding of the functional impact of a disability on a student's ability to perform tasks needed to progress toward mastery of goals. For example, a student may have difficulty learning from printed text because of blindness, a learning disability, an attentional disorder, a physical/positioning challenge or some other category of disability. The key is to recognize that the functional concern is gaining or using information from printed text. The solutions will be different depending upon why the student cannot gain or use information from printed text, but the functional barrier needs to be recognized before it can be lowered.

- **The least complex intervention that will lower barriers to participation and achievement should be a first consideration.**

  "Least complex" does not necessarily mean "simple." If the barriers are significant, the least complex solution to lower them still may be very complex. However, barriers can be created if students are expected to use more complicated technology than is needed. The key is not to make tasks harder for students by requiring them to use technology for something they can do reasonably well without technology or expecting them to use tools that are more complex than required.

- **Operating guidelines are needed to support systematic problem analysis and solution-seeking.**

    The development and use of operating guidelines will help increase a team's ability to assist students with the selection, acquisition, and use of AT. Such guidelines promote equity and consistency throughout the service areas.

    Written operating guidelines and policies include questions that can be answered only at the program level. That is because many local factors, such as financial resources, personnel resources, geography, and educational practices differ between districts and between buildings within a district. To be useful and effective, AT procedures must be a good fit with local resources and local practices, but they don't have to be complicated or separate from other procedures and processes. In fact, it is helpful to everyone involved if the guidelines are an integral part of the program's day-to-day operation.

    Operating guidelines also make it less likely that there will be conflict about AT decisions and implementation. When everyone on an IEP or Individualized Family Service Plan (IFSP) team has a clear picture of what will be done for a student and how and when it will be done, it is easier to track progress, identify what needs to happen, and make sure it does happen.

Using the *QIAT Companion*

While statutory and regulatory language requires that AT devices and services be provided, there is generally a gap between understanding what must be done and knowing how to do it. The *QIAT Companion* will help close that gap by providing practical, how-to information that will guide educators and families as they work together to fulfill AT-related responsibilities. It includes legal responsibilities as well as the practical steps needed to ensure that the consideration, selection, acquisition, and use of AT devices and services are of high quality and are relevant and useful to students who require them. It provides concise, easy references to information needed in each area of AT provision. It can be used with confidence by schools and families as they work through the various phases of AT services for an individual student, or across a school, district, region, or program. Using this resource will enable teams to more fully understand the multiple factors that influence the provision of high-quality AT services and the various roles and responsibilities they must fulfill in order to provide these services on a consistent basis.

The *QIAT Companion* is arranged in eight major sections that align to the eight indicator areas included in *Quality Indicators for Assistive Technology: A Comprehensive Guide to Assistive Technology Services (2015)*. These areas are specific to the actions and responsibilities involved in providing quality AT services. Each area also includes resources and a sample form to guide the process, which can be adapted as needed.

The following is a brief description of each indicator area to clarify its purpose.

- **Quality Indicators for Assistive Technology Consideration** address the special factors for IEP teams to consider during the development of the IEP, as mandated by the Individuals with Disabilities Education Act (IDEA). In most instances, these quality indicators are also appropriate for the consideration of AT for students who are not served under IDEA but who qualify for services under other legislation (e.g., Section 504 of the Rehabilitation Act, Americans with Disabilities Act).

- **Quality Indicators for Assessment of Assistive Technology** are used by a team to identify the devices, services, strategies, and other supports needed to address a student's individual needs. Among other requirements, this section speaks to the IDEA mandate that an AT evaluation must include a functional evaluation conducted in the student's customary environments.

- **Quality Indicators for Including AT in the IEP** focus on the process that takes place in the IEP meeting and the information that is included in the IEP document. These indicators help IEP teams describe the ways AT will be implemented in the student's educational program.

- **Quality Indicators for Assistive Technology Implementation** address how the AT devices and services included in the IEP are provided. They emphasize the importance of people working together to support the student, including using AT to accomplish the tasks necessary to make progress on IEP goals in the general education curriculum and for active participation in customary environments.

- **Quality Indicators for Evaluation of Effectiveness** describe how to determine and document changes in student performance through the collection and analysis of meaningful data. These indicators help teams think about ways to share responsibilities, gather and analyze data, and make data-based decisions.

- **Quality Indicators for Assistive Technology Transition** address how sending and receiving environments work together to ensure that a student's AT devices and services are successfully transferred from one setting to another.

- **Quality Indicators for AT Professional Development and Training** point out critical aspects of increasing the knowledge and skills of educators, families, and students in a variety of AT-related areas such as collaborative processes; a continuum of tools, strategies, and services; resources; legal issues; action planning; and data collection and analysis.

- **Quality Indicators for Administrative Support of Assistive Technology** identify factors critical to developing and sustaining effective, efficient AT services across the school, district, region, or program. This includes activities such as written guidelines, job descriptions, and program evaluation, which can only be accomplished if supported by educational administrators.

The *QIAT Companion* also includes supporting appendices. The appendices augment the quality indicators with intent statements and common errors, self-evaluation matrices, summary sheets, and detailed legal information related to assistive technology. Using these materials, teams can determine their areas of strength and weakness, develop improvement plans, and monitor their progress over time.

Several features used throughout the *QIAT Companion* can be helpful to readers:

- Quality indicators for each area are listed in their entirety at the beginning of each chapter.

- Quality indicators are interdependent; no sequence is implied in the listing.

- The main idea of each quality indicator is bolded when it appears in the discussion.

- The order of the main ideas in the discussion does not necessarily match the order in which the quality indicators appear at the beginning of the chapter. If using the digital edition of this resource, each chapter can be downloaded separately.

The *QIAT Companion* provides educators, families, and other decision-makers with the information they need to work together to ensure that students who may require AT devices and services have what they need to learn and grow. Users may also wish to consult *Quality Indicators for Assistive Technology: A Comprehensive Guide to Assistive Technology Services* for more extensive information on the quality indicators and accompanying intent statements, guiding documents, numerous examples, self-evaluation tools, and in-depth case studies, which will deepen understanding. Selections of this information can also be found at no charge on the QIAT website at *http://qiat.org*.

Reference

The QIAT Leadership Team. (2015). *Quality indicators for assistive technology: A comprehensive guide to assistive technology services*. Wakefield, MA: CAST Professional Publishing.

CHAPTER 1

Quality Indicators for Consideration of Assistive Technology

1. Assistive technology devices and services are *considered for all students with disabilities* regardless of type or severity of disability.

2. During the development of an individualized educational program, every IEP team consistently uses a *collaborative decision-making process* that supports systematic consideration of each student's possible need for assistive technology devices and services.

3. IEP team members have the *collective knowledge and skills* needed to make informed assistive technology decisions and seek assistance when needed.

4. Decisions regarding the need for assistive technology devices and services are *based on the student's IEP goals and objectives, access to curricular and extracurricular activities, and progress in the general education curriculum.*

5. The IEP team *gathers and analyzes data* about the student, customary environments, educational goals, and tasks when considering a student's need for assistive technology devices and services.

6. When assistive technology is needed, the IEP team *explores a range* of assistive technology devices, services, and other supports that address identified needs.

7. The assistive technology consideration process and *results are documented in the IEP* and include a rationale for the decision and supporting evidence.

Ensuring Quality in Assistive Technology Consideration

Assistive technology (AT) devices and services provide students with disabilities with opportunities for increased participation and improved outcomes by enabling them to engage in tasks that would otherwise be difficult or impossible for them due to their disability. For this reason, the Individuals with Disabilities Education Act (IDEA) includes AT devices and services as one of the five special factors that *must be considered for all students who qualify for special education, regardless of the disability category under which they receive services or the severity of the student's needs* during the development and revision of their Individualized Education Program (IEP). Consideration of these factors is intended to ensure that students have the supports and services they need to receive a free appropriate public education (FAPE).

34 C.F.R. § 300.324 DEVELOPMENT, REVIEW, AND REVISION OF IEP

(a) Development of IEP—

(2) Consideration of special factors. The IEP must—

(i) In the case of a child whose behavior impedes the child's learning or that of others, consider the use of positive behavioral interventions and supports, and other strategies, to address that behavior;

(ii) In the case of a child with limited English proficiency, consider the language need of the child as those needs relate to the child's IEP;

(iii) In the case of a child who is blind or visually impaired, provide for **instruction in Braille and the use of Braille** unless the IEP Team determines, after an evaluation of the child's reading and writing skills, needs, and appropriate reading and writing media (including an evaluation of the child's future needs for instruction in Braille or the use of Braille), that instruction in Braille or the use of Braille is not appropriate for the child;

(iv) Consider the **communication needs** of the child, and in the case of a child who is deaf or hard of hearing, consider the child's language and communication needs, opportunities for direction communications with peers and professional personnel in the child's language and communication mode, academic level, and full range of needs, including opportunities for direct instruction in the child's language and communication mode; and

(v) Consider whether the child needs **assistive technology devices and services**.

(Authority: 20-U.S.C. 1414 (d)(3)(B))

(Emphasis added)

Although AT is called out as a separate special factor, it is also related to two other special factors: braille and communication. For a student who is blind or visually impaired, consideration of the need for instruction and use of braille includes how the student will generate braille, access braille files, and read braille, which typically involve AT. For the student who needs communication supports, the IEP team considers what is needed for spoken words and written text. Solutions for written text could be found in the form of accessible educational materials, such as large print, but could also be technology-based, such as using digital text with screen readers. For all students, the IEP team considers whether AT devices and services are needed for participation and achievement.

Central to consideration is the question, "Does the student require AT to make progress toward their IEP goals, access curricular and extracurricular activities, or progress in the general education curriculum?" This chapter addresses issues that impact each IEP team's consideration of a student's possible need for AT devices and services.

The Consideration Process

Each team's decision about the need for AT is based on a student's unique abilities and needs, and takes into account the tasks the student needs to accomplish in various settings. In the IEP meeting, the team engages in a relatively brief discussion to determine one of three outcomes:

- Yes, the student needs AT and what is needed is documented in the IEP

- No, AT is not needed at this time because the student is making satisfactory progress. Discussion is documented in the IEP

- More information is needed in order to make a decision, and steps for further action are developed. Further action might include plans for a trial period of equipment already available in the classroom or school, further in-depth assessment of the student's skills and abilities, referral to a content area specialist within the district, request for assistance from the district AT team, or referral to an AT expert in another agency. Individual states or districts may have specific guidelines for follow up.

Having Collective Knowledge and Skills

Together, the members of the IEP team have the **collective knowledge and skills** to deliberate about AT for that student—or proactively seek such knowledge and skills in the form of training, technical assistance, and/or access to a knowledgeable resource person. No one person knows everything needed to make informed AT decisions. Each member provides critical information from his or her unique perspective. The regular education teacher knows the curriculum, schedule, activities, and technology being used in the general education classroom and provides information about how the student participates. The special education teacher understands special education goals, strategies to support inclusion, and accommodations to support students with disabilities that may include additional technology. The administrator ensures that the right participants are available to support consideration of and subsequent access to AT devices and services. The student and family members contribute knowledge about the student such as how tasks are completed, what accommodations and supports are being used successfully outside of school, and what devices have been used previously.

Gathering and Analyzing Data

The IEP team members **gather and analyze information** about the student's current academic and functional performance in the school, home, and community environments, which they bring to the meeting. They look at the full range of educational and community settings (e.g., classroom, cafeteria, playground, field trips) and think about what it means for a student to be actively involved in each setting. They think about the typical tasks in each setting and how the student completes them.

Making Decisions Regarding the Provision of AT Devices and Services

Central to consideration is the question: *"Does the student require AT to make progress towards IEP goals, participate in extracurricular activities, or access the general education curriculum?"* Some indications that AT may be needed include a lack of progress on previous IEP goals, an increased workload in areas where the student is already struggling, or student frustration with not being able to complete tasks in a timely manner.

If the student is not able to participate in school activities with independence, fluency, and/or accuracy, the team **explores a range of technologies** that may meet the student's needs and abilities and enables the student to participate in learning. More than one technology solution may be considered since there may be a variety of tasks or activities in different settings in which the student has the opportunity for participation. Sometimes these might be simple AT solutions (e.g., pencil grip, slant board, communication board) or more complex technologies (e.g., word processing app on a tablet, voice output communication aid, braille note-taker). The team also considers what **services and supports** are needed to ensure that the student will be able to use the AT to accomplish tasks. Training on the use of the AT for the student, family, and educators that support the effective use of the chosen AT may be needed.

Documenting Consideration Outcomes

Once the IEP team has determined that (1) AT is needed, (2) AT is not needed, or (3) more information is needed and action steps have been defined, and the IEP team **documents the consideration process and the outcome in the IEP**. In all three cases, documentation of the team's deliberations is vital so that future IEP teams and implementers can understand the rationale for AT decisions.

Next Steps

To promote consistency and clarity, education agencies and programs develop a consistent process to consider AT in every IEP meeting and provide agency-wide training on the procedures. Protocols such as the "QIAT Planning Document: Consideration of the Need for AT" included at the end of this chapter can be a helpful model for the AT consideration process.

Resources

The following resources support the content of this chapter.

Guides

- ***Assistive Technology Resource Guide*** *http://www.gpat.org/Georgia-Project-for-Assistive-Technology/Pages/Considering-Assistive-Technology-for-Students-with-Disabilities.aspx*

    This resource guide, developed by the Georgia Project for Assistive Technology (GPAT), provides a framework for thinking about the specific tasks within an instructional area and the types of strategies and devices that can help students. This page also contains other AT consideration resources.

- ***Assistive Technology Consideration Process Guide*** (*http://www.gpat.org/Georgia-Project-for-Assistive-Technology/Pages/Considering-Assistive-Technology-for-Students-with-Disabilities.aspx#Guide*).

    This process guide, developed by the GPAT, provides a framework for considering AT and the critical elements to be addressed.

- ***Minnesota Department of Education Assistive Technology Manual Update (2019)*** (*https://education.mn.gov/MDE/dse/sped/tech/index.htm*).

    This manual, developed by the Division of Special Education, Minnesota Department of Education, includes supports and scaffolds to support the process of consideration by multiple team members, including educators, parents, and students.

Forms

- ***SETT Scaffold for Consideration of AT Needs*** (*http://www.joyzabala.com/uploads/Zabala_SETT_Scaffold_Consideration.pdf*).

    This form, developed by Joy Zabala, Ed.D., outlines a consideration process that begins with decisions about functional areas of concern and gathers information about a student's abilities and needs in those areas. Other resources and forms can also be found at *http://www.joyzabala.com*.

Training

- ***AT Consideration in the IEP Process*** (*www.atinternetmodules.org*).

    This module is a part of the Assistive Technology Internet Modules (ATIM) developed by the Ohio Center for Autism and Low Incidence (OCALI) and partners. It is available through the AT Internet Modules website. This module provides information to IEP teams as they consider AT in the IEP process.

- The Texas 4-Step Model: Considering Assistive Technology in the IEP Process (*http://www.texasat.net/training-modules/consideration-module*)

    This module, developed by the Texas Assistive Technology Network (TATN), can be used to provide learning opportunities on how to consider possible AT needs during the development of the IEP.

QIAT Planning Document: Consideration of the Need for AT

Student: _____

Student ID: _____ Birthdate: _____

School: _____

Participants: _____

Date: _____

IEP teams may use this form to guide discussion and determine if assistive technology devices and/or services are necessary for the student to make progress in IEP goals and curricular tasks.

INSTRUCTIONAL AREA	COMPLETES TASKS WITH ACCOMMODATIONS/ MODIFICATIONS AND/OR ASSISTIVE TECHNOLOGY		CONSIDERATION OUTCOMES—DOCUMENT OUTCOME IN THE IEP
Column A ❏ Initial IEP ❏ Annual IEP Based on the student's previous performance or IEP goals and objectives, check the curricular area(s) or tasks in which the student is not making progress. ❏ Reading ❏ Written Expression ❏ Handwriting ❏ Computer Access ❏ Oral Communication ❏ Math ❏ Activities of Daily Living ❏ Behavior ❏ Transition ❏ Other ❏ Student is making adequate progress Go to column C. ❏ Student is not making adequate progress Go to column B I.	**Column B I** What accommodations and/or modifications have been tried? 1) 2) 3) Results of above: 1) 2) 3) Circle the above accommodations and modifications currently being used. ❏ Student is making adequate progress with current accommodations/modifications. Go to Column C. ❏ Student is not making adequate progress with current accommodations or modifications. List other accommodations or modifications to explore: ❏ No accommodations and modifications have been tried. Go to column B II.	**Column B II** What assistive technology has been tried? 1) 2) 3) Results of above: 1) 2) 3) Circle the above assistive technology tools that are currently being used. ❏ Student is making adequate progress with current assistive technology. Go to Column C. ❏ Student is not making adequate progress with current assistive technology. List features of assistive technology needed: ❏ No assistive technologies have been tried. Go to column C.	**Column C** ❏ Student independently accomplishes tasks in all instructional areas. No assistive technology is required. ❏ Student accomplishes tasks in all instructional areas with current accommodations and modifications. No assistive technology is required. ❏ Student accomplishes tasks in all instructional areas with currently available assistive technology. Assistive technology is required. ❏ Student does not successfully accomplish tasks in all instructional areas. Additional solutions including assistive technology may be required. (Document the nature of the assistance that is needed and follow agency procedures.) Take following action: _____ _____ _____

CHAPTER 2

Quality Indicators for Assessment of Assistive Technology Needs

1. *Procedures* for all aspects of assistive technology assessment are clearly defined and consistently applied.

2. Assistive technology assessments are conducted by a team with the collective knowledge and skills needed to determine possible assistive technology solutions that address the needs and abilities of the student, demands of the customary environments, educational goals, and related activities.

3. All assistive technology assessments include a functional assessment in the student's customary environments, such as the classroom, lunchroom, playground, home, community setting, or work place.

4. Assistive technology assessments, including needed trials, are completed within reasonable timelines.

5. Recommendations from assistive technology assessments are based on data about the student, environments, and tasks.

6. The assessment provides the IEP team with clearly documented recommendations that guide decisions about the selection, acquisition, and use of assistive technology devices and services.

7. Assistive technology needs are reassessed any time changes in the student, the environments, and/or the tasks result in the student's needs not being met with current devices and/or services

Ensuring Quality Assistive Technology Assessment Services

The Quality Indicators for the Assessment of Assistive Technology Needs highlight the need for education agencies and programs to have **procedures** in place that enable them to consistently provide effective, efficient assistive technology (AT) assessments across the agency or program. When developing assessment procedures, agencies and programs must address the critical elements across all assessment components, including making referrals, planning and conducting assessment processes, and developing reports.

Note that, in this resource and in the book, *Quality Indicators for Assistive Technology: A Comprehensive Guide to Assistive Technology Service,* the term *assistive technology assessment* is synonymous with the term *assistive technology evaluation* referenced in 34 C.F.R. § 300.6 Assistive technology services. (See the "Legal References" section in Appendix D at the end of the *QIAT Companion*.)

The Assessment Process

An assistive technology assessment typically takes place under one or more of two conditions: 1) When more information is needed for the IEP Team to make a decision about whether or not a student requires assistive technology devices and services; or 2) when more information is needed to determine the features of AT devices and the extent of AT services needed by a student.

Making the Referral

Educators, students, or family members can request an AT assessment. The referral needs to address the specific questions the assessment will be designed to answer, such as the following:

- How does the student's disability affect their access to the general curriculum and their academic and functional performance?
- What tasks are difficult or impossible for the student to accomplish with the technology, materials, and supports provided to all students?
- What environmental barriers affect the student's performance?
- What AT, if any, is currently in use and how well is it working?

Forming the Assessment Team

A successful assessment process is carried out by a team of people who **collectively have the necessary knowledge and ability.** The assessment team is built around the needs of the student. The team includes the student, the family, and relevant professionals who are knowledgeable about the student's customary environments and the potential barriers the student encounters. The AT assessment team will typically include the following:

- People who are knowledgeable about the student's strengths, interests, needs, customary environments, and potential barriers.

- Someone who knows the relevant curriculum (e.g., grade level, alternative learning standards) and the academic and social expectations put on the student; this is usually the student's general education teacher and/or special education teacher.

- Someone who knows the student's language, sensory, or motor needs, if necessary; this may be the student's speech language pathologist, occupational or physical therapist, or a teacher.

- Someone knowledgeable about AT devices and services who can make appropriate recommendations for the student.

Establishing Timelines

An AT assessment and necessary trials must be conducted within a **reasonable timeline**. It is the Individualized Education Program (IEP) team's responsibility to set a timeline that will enable them to determine what AT devices and services the student might need. The timeline must include a trial period that is long enough to give the student sufficient opportunity to use the tools so the team can determine the impact of the tools on the student's achievement. In some cases, this may become apparent in a few days or weeks, whereas other students may need more time to become familiar with the device and demonstrate that it improves their achievement.

Gathering Information from Multiple Sources

To prepare for an AT assessment, the team reviews the questions that the assessment will address. The team determines the scope of the assessment based on the complexity of the questions about the student's performance and develops an assessment plan that includes:

- questions to be addressed during the assessment;

- assessment activities needed to address the questions;

- what will be measured and how it will be measured;

- assigned responsibilities; and

- a specific and *reasonable timeline.*

Once the assessment plan has been established and parental permission for AT assessment has been obtained, team members proceed with specific steps to gather relevant data. Data may include the student's unique abilities and needs, the demands of the customary environments in which the student participates, the educational tasks related to the general education curriculum, and the student's special education goals and objectives. This may include the following:

- Having a discussion that includes the student, family, teachers, and service providers;
- Reviewing the student's records, including special education records and previous assessments;
- Observing in the **classroom and other customary environments** to determine important aspects of the student's academic and functional performance, and critical elements in those environments (e.g., lighting, sound, location of teacher, location of student, type of instructional activity, distractions, typical behavior during routine tasks and activities);
- Conducting or reviewing formal or informal assessment activities that might be useful; and
- Reviewing any previous trials with AT and general instructional technology that is used in the classroom.

Conducting Trials and Analyzing Data

The AT assessment team conducts trials to try out AT devices and strategies and evaluate their effectiveness. Steps for conducting the trials and analyzing data may include the following:

- Reviewing the information gathered across customary environments
- Identifying the features needed for any AT that should be tried with the student
- Choosing specific AT devices for trials
- Deciding upon levels of support to be provided during the trial
- Arranging for the AT devices to be available
- Setting timelines for trials and detailing how and when they will take place
- Assigning staff responsibilities
- Conducting the trials
- Collecting the results of trials
- Analyzing the cumulative data

Making and Documenting Recommendations

Recommendations **based on data** about the student, customary environments, and tasks are **made and clearly documented** to guide decisions about the selection, acquisition, and use of AT devices. Documentation also includes recommendations about the AT services needed to support the effective use of the technology. The written report includes a rationale for the AT recommendations that will help the student's team, the classroom teacher, and the family implement the AT as suggested. The assessment report includes the following:

- Reason for the assessment
  - **questions** that led to the assessment
  - **current** barriers to performance
  - **information** on AT currently in use and how it is working, if applicable
- Process for the assessment
  - **specific** tasks conducted by the AT assessment team
  - **location** and conditions of assessment activities
  - **accommodations,** interventions, and strategies, including features of the AT used during the assessment
  - **specific** features of the AT devices identified as important and the settings or tasks in which they were most effective
  - **changes** in the student's performance when using the AT that are evident from the data collected
- Summary
  - **recommended** AT devices and services, accommodations, interventions, and strategies
  - **training** needs of the staff, student, and family members
  - **other** information the assessment team determines to be necessary for effective implementation of the recommended AT

Requesting Reassessment

If the AT a student is currently using is no longer meeting the student's needs or if conditions have changed, a ***reassessment*** may be needed to provide new recommendations so that the student continues to succeed academically and functionally. Changes in student performance, the demands of the environment, or the complexity and difficulty of the tasks the student needs to complete may signal the need for a reassessment.

Seeking Outside Assistance

In some cases, the district may want to use the services of an outside consultant or agency to conduct or assist with an AT assessment. This may occur if specific circumstances require additional support or specialized skills. When contracting with an individual or agency to conduct or participate in an AT assessment, the responsibilities of the referring education agency (i.e., the school or program) include the following:

- providing access to the student in customary environments,
- developing specific referral questions for the evaluation and the procedure for communicating these questions to the contractor(s), and
- determining the role referring team members will play in the assessment, including working with the contracted evaluator(s) to complete the assessment tasks and conducting any trials needed in the student's customary environments.

Although not binding, the findings of any contracted evaluation will add to the data already collected by the student's team. Findings will be considered in the IEP team's final determination of whether or not the student needs AT and, if so, what AT devices and services will be provided.

Next Steps

To promote clarity and consistency in the assessment process, schools and programs may find it helpful to develop planning forms that guide AT assessment processes. Using forms to guide the process can help teams provide effective, efficient AT assessments that are consistent across the agency or program. One useful form is the QIAT Assistive Technology Assessment Process Planner, included at the end of this chapter. The resource section includes other forms that are widely used to support the assessment process.

Resources

The following resources support the content of this chapter.

Forms

- ***Wisconsin Assistive Technology Initiative (WATI) Assessment Package***
  (*http://www.wati.org/free-publications/assistive-technology-consideration-to-assessment*).

  This set of forms was originally developed by the WATI staff and was updated recently. It includes the "Procedure Guide for Assessment," "Student Information Guide," "Environmental Observation Guide," "Tool Identification Guide," "AT Decision Making Guide," "AT Continuums," "Trial Use Guide," and "Trial Use Summary" as both printable and fillable forms.

- **SETT** (*HYPERLINK "http://www.joyzabala.com" http://www.joyzabala.com*).

The SETT Scaffolds were developed by Joy Zabala, Ed.D. They include the "SETT Scaffold for Data Gathering," "SETT Scaffold for Tool Selection," and "SETT Scaffold for Implementation and Evaluation of Effectiveness Planning."

Training

- ***The Assistive Technology Internet Modules (ATIM)*** (*http://www.atinternetmodules.org/*).

    These modules, developed by the Ohio Center for Autism and Low Incidence (OCALI) and their partners, are available through the AT Internet Modules website. They cover a wide variety of topics and include the series, "Using the WATI Assessment Process."

- ***POWER AAC Modules*** (*https://www.pattan.net/Assistive-Technology/AT-for-Communication/POWER-AAC*).

    These modules, designed by Pennsylvania Training and Technical Assistance Network (PaTTAN), are intended to build the capacity of those serving students with complex communication needs who may require augmentative and alternative communication (AAC) systems. The materials are appropriate for self-directed use or for use by a professional learning community.

- ***PrAACtical AAC*** (*http://praacticalaac.org/?s=assessment*).

    PrAACtical AAC was founded in 2011 by two speech language pathologists, Carole Zangari and the late Robin Parker, around their shared passion for AAC. It supports a community of professionals and families who are determined to improve the communication and literacy abilities of people with significant communication difficulties.

Report Writing

- ***The AAC Report Coach*** (*http://aacfundinghelp.com/report_coach.html*).

    The "AAC Report Coach," developed by Pam Mathy, PhD, offers SLPs and their teams a guide to writing a funding report to support an AAC recommendation.

Assistive Technology Assessment Process Planner

Student Name: _____ Planning Date: _____

	By Date	Person
Referral for AT assessment is made by any member of the student's team when classroom strategies and tools do not meet the student's needs.		
AT assessment is completed by a collaborative team sharing responsibilities		
Determine team members		
Create a written AT assessment plan including:		
Determine the assessment question(s)		
Identify expected results & outcomes (e.g., Student will be able to____)		
Determine what will be measured (e.g., speed, quantity, quality, rate, accuracy, endurance)		
Assign responsibilities		
Set a timeline		
Gather information from multiple sources including previous information (e.g., educational reports, assessments, background interviews, and other records)		
Student's strengths		
Student's needs		
Environmental expectations		
Tasks (e.g., required curricular work, testing, homework, projects, in-class work, materials, statewide testing, & other school functions)		
Current levels of performance for identified tasks (baseline data)		
Barriers to participation & independence		
Analyze information to identify tools & strategies for the trials		
Determine the features needed		
Choose tools with appropriate features		
Determine source of trials from demos, loaners, & rental programs		
Set timelines		
Prepare data collection recording method (measurable determined above)		
Conduct the trials with identified tools		
Have student use tools in customary environment for identified tasks		
Collect data		

	By Date	Person
Analyze Data		
Report the results of the trials		
Revisit the assessment question(s) to determine the outcomes		
Determine the most appropriate tool(s) & strategies or if additional trials are necessary		
Document recommendations in written form following district assistive technology procedural guidelines		
Summarize student performance while using AT tools, including tools that were and were not successful		
Document appropriate tools and potential impact on student achievement		
If needed, include specific language for procurement of AT, and possible funding sources (Refer to Quality Indicator for Administrative Support for AT)		
Document required tools & strategies in student's plan (e.g., IEP, 504 Plan) (Refer to Quality Indicator for Documentation in the IEP)		
Develop implementation plan		
Instructional/access areas which were explored during the trial		
Summary of specific skills assessed		
Written action plan including team member roles & responsibilities (refer to Quality Indicator for AT Implementation)		
Reassess as needs change		
Monitor the student abilities, environment, tasks, and barriers as well as effectiveness of current AT on an ongoing basis		

CHAPTER 3

Quality Indicators for Including Assistive Technology in the IEP

1. The education agency has *guidelines for documenting* assistive technology needs in the IEP and requires their consistent application.

2. All *services* that the IEP team determines are needed to support the selection, acquisition, and use of assistive technology devices are designated in the IEP.

3. The IEP illustrates that assistive technology is a *tool to support achievement of goals* and progress in the general curriculum by establishing a clear relationship between student needs, assistive technology devices and services, and the student's goals and objectives.

4. IEP content regarding assistive technology use is written in language that describes how assistive technology contributes to achievement of *measurable and observable outcomes.*

5. Assistive technology is included in the IEP in a manner that provides a *clear and complete description* of the devices and services to be provided and used to address student needs and achieve expected results.

Ensuring Quality When Including Assistive Technology in the IEP

The Individualized Education Program (IEP) is the foundation of a student's educational program and provides all who work with the student with a roadmap for implementation. The IEP is both a document that describes the services the student will receive and a process that enables educators, families, and the student to work together to develop the individualized plan. The Individuals with Disabilities Education Act (IDEA) states that, if a student needs assistive technology (AT) devices and services as a part of special education, related services, or supplementary aids and services to receive a free appropriate public education (FAPE), those devices and services must be provided at no cost to the family.

To ensure that AT devices and services are provided and used, the IEP document must contain a **clear and complete description** of the devices and services that address student needs. A well-developed IEP illustrates that AT is used as a **tool to support achievement of goals** and progress in the general curriculum by establishing a relationship between student needs, AT devices and services, and the student's goals as well as relevant objectives and benchmarks.

Team members often ask exactly where in the IEP AT devices and services should be documented and how such documentation should be worded. To ensure that documentation of AT devices and services promotes understanding by all who will be implementing the IEP, schools and programs develop **guidelines for documenting** AT devices and services in the IEP. Guidelines will also help ensure that documentation includes the **services needed to support the selection, acquisition, and use of AT** devices. IEP content addressing AT is most useful when it clearly describes how AT devices and services contribute to **achievement of goals** and **observable, measurable outcomes**.

Including AT in the IEP Process

There are several places in the IEP where the need for and use of AT devices and services are logically included, and each will be expanded upon in the following sections:

- "Summary of Evaluation Results"
- "Present Levels of Academic Achievement and Functional Performance"
- "Special Factors"
- "Measurable Annual Goals"
- "Related Services"
- "Supplementary Aids and Services"
- "Program Modifications and Supports for School Personnel"

- "Participation in Statewide Assessments"
- "Postsecondary Goals and Transition Services"

Basic Principles

As the team works through each of these areas of IEP development, two principles apply broadly to all documentation of AT in the IEP.

First, it is considered good practice *not* to include the brand names of AT hardware, software, and apps in the IEP. Instead, provide a robust, generic description of the needed device(s) and the specific features that the student will use to make progress toward mastery of goals. For example, one might write "tablet computer with word prediction" instead of *"name of device* with *name of program or/application."* (A suggested exception to this practice will be discussed in the section "Present Levels of Academic Achievement and Functional Performance.")

Second, even when hardware, software, and/or apps are readily available in current environments for use by all students, they need to be included in a student's IEP if they are essential for that student to access the curriculum and work toward goals. This way, when environments or other circumstances change, the IEP provides a complete record of what the student needs.

Summary of Evaluation Results

Evaluation is a critical first step toward ensuring that a student has the supports needed for educational participation and progress. If evaluation information suggests that AT devices and services are needed to support a student's access to participation and instruction, that information is documented in this section of the IEP. The following are examples of information that may be relevant to include

- barriers to the student's participation and progress on the special education goals and in the general education curriculum; or,
- findings and recommendations that help the IEP team determine that the student either needs AT to lower identified barriers or AT is not needed at the current time.

Present Levels of Academic Achievement and Functional Performance

If a student is currently using AT devices and services to participate and make progress in the general curriculum and on IEP goals, documentation in this section should include how the AT contributes to the student's present levels of achievement and performance by addressing

- the specific AT the student is using,
- the tasks for which the student uses AT,
- the ways the AT contributes to the student's ability to complete the tasks, and
- the environments in which the AT is being used.

Although, as noted, it is generally considered good practice not to include the brand names of AT hardware, software, and apps in the IEP, it could be useful here to name the specific technology and the features the student uses to reach the levels described. For example, "James can read and understand grade-level materials across the curriculum when he is provided with digital materials and text-to-speech software. He has a Bookshare account and is a proficient user of the Bookshare Web Reader on the iPad that he uses independently in all of his classes. He also uses a read-aloud feature on the iPad to read digital text." This information will help the team decide whether the current technology is sufficient or whether something different is needed.

Implementers will also benefit from knowing what specific product the student has been using when a student moves to using a new product with similar features, since a change in student performance could be due to becoming familiar with the new product. This information would also be important if the student moves to a new environment where students transition to using similar (but not the same) products as they did before.

If the student is not currently using AT, the present levels may suggest key areas that the team might consider in determining whether AT could improve the student's achievement. For example, a statement such as, "Sarah can understand grade-level content when it is presented to her orally, but cannot decode adequately to read grade-level materials independently" may cue the team to consider the student's need for accessible materials and technologies.

Special Factors

As discussed in Chapter 1, Quality Indicators for Consideration of Assistive Technology," IDEA charges IEP teams with conducting a thorough consideration of a student's need for AT devices and services. The team may consider whether the student needs AT devices and services to

- lower barriers to participation and progress in the general curriculum;
- benefit from specially designed instruction, related services, or supplementary aids and services; and
- complete educationally relevant tasks.

Consideration of the need for AT is also related to two other special factors: braille and communication. If the team determines that the student needs AT for any of these purposes, it documents the need in this section and continues developing the IEP. If team members anticipate that the student will make satisfactory progress toward mastery of IEP goals and in the general curriculum without AT devices and services, they also document that in this section and continue developing the IEP. In some instances, the team may have the opportunity to support their decision with a statement such as, "Evidence indicates that Jason does not currently need AT, but this decision will be reconsidered at future IEP meetings or at any time if data indicate that progress toward goals is not occurring as expected."

Measurable Annual Goals

When AT devices and services are required as a part of a student's special education or for access to the general curriculum, the description of devices and services needed must be clearly connected to the achievement of one or more measurable annual goals.

There are two common ways that AT can be documented in this section. Required AT can be included in the wording of each measurable annual goal for which it is needed, or it can be written in a way that connects the AT to multiple goals. There are strengths and challenges in each of these ways of documenting AT devices and services. If there is state or district guidance that recommends one over the other, follow it so that there is consistency across the organization. When AT is included within each goal for which it is needed, the connection between the AT and the goal is clear and those implementing the student's IEP know exactly what the AT is expected to help the student achieve.

Examples of AT written directly into multiple goals might read:

- Goal 1: Juan will use a tablet computer with word prediction when writing essays in English class.

- Goal 2: Juan will use a tablet computer with word prediction when completing reports on the results of experiments in science class.

When a single statement connects the AT to multiple goals, goals can be written so that it is clear what the student to working to achieve. Not including the means in the goals provides the opportunity for the student to work toward the goals even if, for some reason the specific technology is not available for a short time (e.g., not charged, accidentally left at home, in for repairs).

Building upon the example above, the goals and a single statement that connects AT to multiple goals might read:

- Goal 1: Juan will write essays in English class.

- Goal 2: Juan will complete reports on the results of experiments in science class.

The single statement may read:

When assignments require written productivity of more than a paragraph, Juan will use a tablet computer with word prediction. If the tablet is not available, Juan will temporarily use another means to address this goal (e.g., classroom computer with word prediction, or in an emergency, dictation to a scribe)

Such a statement may be documented as a goal, an accommodation, or in some other section of the IEP.

Related Services

AT devices and services that are needed as part of a related service are documented in this section of the IEP. For example, a student with complex communication needs may require an augmentative communication system as a part of the student's related services. The AT is documented as a part of the related service already being provided by a speech-language pathologist who, most likely, also supports the use of the technology for communication across learning environments. When AT devices and services are provided as a part of a related service, documentation includes the projected date for the beginning of the services, and the anticipated frequency, location, and duration of services.

Supplementary Aids and Services

If a student needs supplementary aids and services to be educated with nondisabled peers to the maximum extent appropriate, they are documented in this section of the IEP. For example, a student in a regular classroom who has physical disabilities may require AT devices and services that enable the student to prepare, participate, interact, and be productive in general education classrooms, other education-related settings, and in extracurricular and nonacademic settings.

Program Modifications and Supports for School Personnel

Program modifications and training supports are discussed and documented in this section of the IEP. As discussed in depth in Chapter 8, "Professional Development and Training" school personnel and family members often need training to support a student using AT. Topics may include

- AT-related training or supports needed by the school personnel working with the student to implement the student's AT;

- training family members need to support the student's use of AT in other environments, including the home;

- occasional or ongoing technical assistance and support needed to help the student use the AT for the purposes for which it is intended; or

- discussion about whether the training needed will be provided by a staff member or outside provider.

Participation in Statewide Assessments

Many students need AT devices and services to participate in large-scale, statewide assessments. Testing accommodations should, to the greatest extent possible, mirror accommodations used in the classroom. Documentation of those needs is included in this section of the IEP. The discussion and exploration may also address

- the student's use of AT devices and services in the classroom for instruction and classroom assessments,

- the parts of statewide assessments where a student's classroom AT devices and services are permitted, or

- whether the AT the student is using is technically compatible with the statewide assessment delivery system.

If the student's typical AT is not allowed on statewide assessments or is technically incompatible with the assessment delivery system, the team explores and documents

- supports that are within or technically compatible with the assessment delivery system that enable the student to show what they know and are able to do, and
- accommodations that will be provided to enable the student to show what they know and are able to do.

Postsecondary Goals and Transition Services

As discussed in Chapter 6, "AT in Transition" the AT devices and services a student needs when making the transition to postsecondary environments are documented in this section of the IEP. The student, family, and representatives of both the sending and the receiving environments work together to explore the following issues and document the results. They include appropriate goals related to

- postsecondary education,
- vocational education,
- employment,
- adult services,
- independent living, and
- community participation

Next Steps

The IEP is the bridge between determining the AT devices and services that a student needs and the implementation of AT within the student's educational program. Consistent use of the information in this chapter can help ensure the provision of equitable, high-quality AT services across the school or program. There are many ways to do it well. Where AT appears in the IEP is not as important as the fact that AT is included in a way that makes sense to those who will be implementing and supporting the student's use of AT. When all involved understand what effective AT implementation looks like and how to evaluate effectiveness, the AT is more likely to be consistently integrated into the student's daily activities. The "QIAT Assistive Technology in the IEP Planner," included at the end of this chapter, offers an example of a form that supports IEP teams as they address AT.

Resources

The following resources support the content of this chapter.

Guides

- ***Assistive Technology in the IEP: A Guide for IEP Teams*** (*https://www.pattan.net/Publications/Assistive-Technology-in-the-IEP-A-Guide-for-IEP-Te*)

  This document provides a brief overview of AT in the IEP for IEP teams in Pennsylvania. The information is also largely applicable to other states.

- ***Writing Assistive Technology in the IEP*** (*https://ataem.org/at-resource-guide/6-writing-at-into-the-iep*).

  This chapter, part of the *Assistive Technology Resource Guide* written by the Ohio Center for Autism and Low Incidence (OCALI) and partners, includes QIAT and provides additional support specific to Ohio that may also be useful to IEP teams in other states.

- ***Assistive Technology and the IEP*** (*https://www.ctdinstitute.org/sites/default/files/file_attachments/AT-IEP-English2_0.pdf*).

  In this guide, the federally funded Center on Technology and Disability provides an overview of the IEP process from the family's point of view.

Video

- ***Documenting AT in the IEP*** (*https://www.youtube.com/watch?v=T6u0zWSTM-k*).

  This video by Oklahoma ABLE Tech discusses how one state has used QIAT to guide the inclusion of AT in the IEP.

Assistive Technology in the IEP Planner

The following questions guide IEP team discussion for considering and documenting AT in the IEP.

QUESTIONS FOR IEP TEAMS:	DOCUMENT IN IEP SECTION:
Does the student currently use AT devices to participate and make progress in the general education curriculum? ■ For what tasks is AT used? ■ Is AT effective in completing these tasks? ■ In what environments is AT used? ■ Are AT services currently being provided? ■ Are there additional tasks for which AT might be effective?	Present Levels of Academic Achievement and Functional Performance
Does the student need AT devices and/or services to accomplish annual goals? ■ How will AT support progress toward annual goals? ■ In what environments will AT be used? ■ Do goals need to be developed that address acquisition of technology related skills?	Measurable Annual Goals (Functional and Academic)
Does the student need AT devices and/or services to accomplish benchmarks and/or short-term objectives? ■ How will AT support progress toward benchmarks and/or short-term objectives? ■ In what environments will AT be used? ■ Do benchmarks and/or short-term goals need to be developed that address acquisition of technology related skills?	Short-term Objectives or Benchmarks
Does the student need AT devices and/or services to participate and progress in the curriculum or to benefit from specially designed instruction? ■ Does the student need AT to remove barriers to participation in the general education curriculum? ■ Does the student need AT to complete educationally relevant tasks?	Consideration of Special Factors
Does the student need AT devices and/or services as part of related services to enable the student to benefit from special education? ■ Will the provision of AT devices or services become part of the services of a current service provider? ■ Will an additional service provider provide the AT services?	Related Services
Does the student need AT devices and/or services as part of supplementary aids and services to support participation in general education classes or other education related settings to enable him or her to be educated with children without disabilities?	Supplementary Aids and Services
Do the school personnel working with the student need any AT-related training or supports? ■ Do school personnel need training to develop and/or implement the student's AT? ■ Do school personnel need technical assistance and support to develop and/or implement the student's AT?	Program Modifications or Supports for School Personnel

(continued)

QUESTIONS FOR IEP TEAMS:	DOCUMENT IN IEP SECTION:
Does the student need AT to participate in state-wide and district assessments? - Is the identified AT a component of the student's typical instruction and/or classroom assessments? - Is the use of identified AT allowed in the assessment? - Is the identified AT available within or compatible with the assessment? - Can the identified AT be used without invalidating the test construct?	Accommodations for Participation in State and District-wide Assessments
Does the student need AT devices and/or services as a part of transition to post-school environments? Does the student need AT devices and/or services to accomplish measurable goals related to: - Post-secondary education - Vocational education - Employment - Adult services - Independent living - Community participation Have AT service providers been identified for post-school environments and invited to participate?	Transition Services

CHAPTER 4

Quality Indicators for the Implementation of Assistive Technology

1. Assistive technology implementation proceeds according to a collaboratively developed plan.

2. Assistive technology is integrated into the curriculum and daily activities of the student across environments.

3. Persons supporting the student across all environments in which the assistive technology is expected to be used share responsibility for implementation of the plan.

4. Persons supporting the student provide opportunities for the student to use a variety of strategies—including assistive technology—and to learn which strategies are most effective for particular circumstances and tasks.

5. Learning opportunities for the student, family, and staff are an integral part of implementation.

6. Assistive technology implementation is initially based on assessment data and is adjusted based on performance data.

7. Assistive technology implementation includes management and maintenance of equipment and materials.

Ensuring Quality Assistive Technology Implementation Services

While implementation is primarily a series of actions that happen after the Individualized Education Program (IEP) meeting, the plan for how to use the assistive technology (AT) selected by or for a student actually begins during assessment. Specific and well-thought-out assessment questions drive the trials that are set up and the acquisition of information derived from the assessment trial data. Once the assessment data is analyzed and the IEP goals are developed, an implementation plan can be developed.

An implementation plan is a written document that includes how the AT will be used in specific settings, what will be done, and who will do it. The plan is as important for students using low-tech strategies and devices as it is for students requiring more robust technology. An effective plan is **developed collaboratively** by all individuals who will be involved in implementation, including the student and their family members. The implementation plan ideally is aligned with a process for evaluating the effectiveness of the AT devices and services being provided. A planning tool, such as the "QIAT Implementation of Assistive Technology Planner" included at the end of this chapter, can be used to support the development of the implementation plan.

The Implementation Process

Effective AT implementation enables students using assistive technology to actively participate in and benefit from curricular and extra-curricular activities. Attention to all aspects of the implementation process increases the likelihood that the use of assistive technology will result in increased student achievement and improved outcomes.

Sharing Responsibility for Implementation

Implementation is a **shared responsibility**. The individuals supporting the student are responsible for providing them with opportunities to use AT. In addition to the team members who were present at the IEP meeting, others not at the meeting but whose input may have been provided in writing, need to be informed of the meeting outcomes. The implementation plan delineates which team members will share responsibility for the actions necessary to implement the IEP. This includes the student and the family, as well as the educational staff. The more input a student provides, the more likely the use of the AT will be effective. If needed, the implementation plan can be adjusted for specific concerns, such as seating, positioning, and device mounting.

Assignment of responsibilities for training, physical setup, relevant content, opportunities for daily use, **maintenance, repair**, and other aspects of AT use need to be included for each of the student's settings throughout the day. **Learning opportunities** for the student and family members are imperative and, if needed, should include solutions determined during the assessment process to be appropriate for the home setting.

Integrating AT into the Curriculum

Assistive technology may facilitate active participation in educational activities, assessments, extracurricular activities, and typical routines. Therefore, it is important that the **AT is integrated** into activities in which the student participates across multiple environments. The goal is for AT to be a part of a **variety of strategies** that the student uses across environments, so it becomes a useful and effective tool for meaningful tasks through regular use. Steps may include

- identifying specific goals and tasks to be addressed, and prioritizing goals for the beginning of the process;
- relating the use of the AT to specific curriculum areas, routines, and coursework;
- pairing possible devices and/or strategies with specific tasks;
- identifying the aspects of the student's performance that are expected to change and in what ways;
- assigning staff roles and responsibilities;
- planning for the collection and analysis of evidence/**data** about the AT's use in order to guide its continued implementation and planning; and
- identifying and providing **learning opportunities** to ensure success for all team members, including the family and the student.

Using the SETT Framework or some other tool to contrast a student's current and expected performance may be helpful in obtaining this detailed information. An activity-objective matrix, like the one seen in Figure 4.1, can be modified to identify which AT strategies are being used to address challenges across the IEP goals and in the general curriculum. This method will keep track of devices and strategies the student tries during the day. It is important to track both low- and high-tech devices and how they are being used in specific situations.

FIGURE 4.1. Sample Activity-Objective Matrix

Name: Mason **Date:** _____

GOALS	ACTIVITIES								
	Arrival	Morning Meeting	Centers	Lang. Arts	Specials	Lunch	Reading	Math	Centers
Greet	X				X	X			
Strategy Used	gesture				gesture	gesture			
Make choices to set schedule	X		X						X
Strategy Used	Choice Board		AAC Device						AAC Device
Request objects/ actions		X		X	X	X			
Strategy Used		AAC Device		AAC Device	AAC Device	AAC Device			
Request help					X		X	X	
Strategies Used					Vocalize		AAC Device	Manual boards	
Comment		X		X				X	X
Strategies Used		none		AAC Device				none	AAC Device
Turn-taking w/ peer			X				X		X
Strategies Used			Gesture				AAC Device		Manual boards

Adapted with permission from the AAC Activity-Objective Matrix published by Praacticalaac.org.

Executing the Plan

Once the plan has been developed and agreed upon, put it into practice. Follow the plan including the timelines and responsibilities. Successful implementation will include the following.

Making the plan available to all team members and keeping it current The team might collaborate with the instructional technology department to find out if an online collaboration tool is available. A group e-mail or low-tech strategies like a notebook in which anyone can jot down notes could also be used to keep everyone informed.

Communicating success and/or the need for changes Data need to be reviewed on a regular basis. The annual IEP team meeting review generally is not often enough for the fine-tuning necessary to achieve success with AT devices and strategies. Weekly, monthly, or quarterly meetings to review progress and make adjustments as needed are critical.

Managing and maintaining devices The steps to be taken will need to be developed and documented, along with who is responsible for each step. Tasks such as charging the device, mounting the AT device, and adding new vocabulary to an AAC system are just a few examples. A back-up plan to be implemented if the original AT is damaged or unavailable is especially important.

Holding team members accountable for appropriately supporting the student's use of AT Establish a routine way that the administrator who supervises the team members will be kept informed to facilitate follow through. Only an administrator can require a team member to take specific actions. The level of positive administrative support a team receives will impact its effectiveness and the outcome of the AT use.

Next Steps

Team members consider the following important components and regularly review how well they are progressing to impact successful AT implementation and the student's educational productivity, participation, and independence.

- They review the *evidence/data* to be collected and the timeline to do so. Implementation is initially based on assessment data and adjusted based on performance data.

- Team members with responsibility for the provision of opportunities for the student to use the AT throughout the day in meaningful activities are carrying out the tasks they were assigned.

- Initial and ongoing *learning opportunities* are being provided for team members.

- Remember to follow-up and follow along with both the student's and staff members' progress and make adjustments as needed.

Teams may use the "QIAT Implementation of Assistive Technology Planner" included at the end of this chapter to guide discussion during the development of an implementation plan that is well thought out and includes input from all stakeholders.

Resources

The following resources support the content of this chapter.

Forms

- **Assistive Technology Planner from IEP Consideration to Classroom Implementation** (*http://natri.uky.edu/atPlannermenu.html*).

    This concise, two-page form developed by the National Assistive Technology Research Institute (NATRI) focuses on the team approach to implementation.

- **Assistive Technology Implementation Plan** (*http://www.gpat.org/Georgia-Project-for-Assistive-Technology/Pages/Implementation-and-Integration.aspx*)

    Developed by the Georgia Project for Assistive Technology (GPAT), this three-page form helps guide teams through the intervention steps, including the integration of all AT used in the relevant environments and activities.

Training

- *Assistive Technology Internet Modules (ATIM)* (*http://www.atinternetmodules.org/*).

    The implementation module is one of many developed by the Ohio Center for Autism and Low Incidence (OCALI) and partners and is made available through the AT Internet Modules website. The module can be utilized for self-study or in a professional learning community.

- *PaTTAN POWER AAC* (*https://www.pattan.net/Assistive-Technology/AT-for-Communication/POWER-AAC*).

    Power AAC is a series of modules developed by PaTTAN with Gail Van Tatenhove to build the capacity of those who serve students with complex communication needs who require the use of AAC systems. The materials are appropriate for self-directed use or use by a professional learning community.

Websites

- ***WATI*** (*http://www.wati.org*)

    The WATI website includes many resources, for example forms developed as assessment tools in areas such as assistive technology use, communication, writing, computer access, and other valuable resources to use when planning for implementation.

- ***SETT*** (*http://www.joyzabala.com*)

    The SETT Scaffolds were developed by Joy Zabala, Ed.D., and the website includes sample forms to support data gathering, tool selection, and implementation and evaluation of effectiveness planning.

- ***PrAACtical AAC*** (*http://praacticalaac.org/?s=implementation+plan*)

    PrAACtical AAC supports a community of professionals and families who are determined to improve the communication and literacy abilities of people with significant communication difficulties. It was founded in 2011 by two speech-language pathologists, Carole Zangari and the late Robin Parker, around a shared passion for augmentative and alternative communication (AAC). The website offers many resources including the article, "Boosting AAC Implementation in the Classroom: 6 Things to Try," which provides strategies to encourage all team members to participate in the implementation process.

Implementation of Assistive Technology Planner

Teams may use this form to guide discussion in the development of an implementation plan that is well thought-out with input from all stakeholders (team members). Best practices suggest that all components below should be considered when developing the AT implementation plan.

KEY ELEMENTS OF AN AT IMPLEMENTATION PLAN
Who will collaborate in the development of the implementation plan?
What specific goals and tasks will be addressed in the plan?
What aspects of the student's performance are expected to change (e.g., reduced time, increased accuracy, quantity, quality, engagement)?
How will AT be integrated into the curriculum and daily activities across environments?
What tools and strategies will be used to accomplish identified tasks?
What evidence/data will be needed to determine which tools and strategies are most effective for particular environments and tasks?
How will performance evidence/data be measured and collected?
When will the performance evidence/data be reviewed to determine what changes, if any, are needed in the implementation plan?
What do team members need to do for successful implementation to take place?
Which team members (e.g., staff, family, supporters, student) will share responsibility for each action that needs to be taken?
What initial and ongoing learning opportunities will be provided for all team members, including the student?
How will equipment and materials be managed and maintained?

CHAPTER 5

Quality Indicators for Evaluation of Effectiveness of Assistive Technology

1. Team members share *clearly defined responsibilities* to ensure that data are collected, evaluated, and interpreted by capable and credible team members.

2. Evaluation data are collected on specific student achievement that has been identified by the team and is *related to one or more goals.*

3. Evaluation of effectiveness includes the *quantitative and qualitative measurement of changes* in the student's performance and achievement.

4. Effectiveness is evaluated *across environments* during naturally occurring and structured activities.

5. Data are collected to provide teams with a means for *analyzing student achievement and identifying supports and barriers* that influence assistive technology use to determine what changes, if any, are needed.

6. *Changes are made* in the student's assistive technology services and educational program when evaluation data indicate that such changes are needed to improve student achievement.

7. Evaluation of effectiveness is a dynamic, responsive, *ongoing process* that is reviewed periodically.

Ensuring Quality When Evaluating the Effectiveness of Assistive Technology

Evaluating the effectiveness of a student's assistive technology (AT) use and the *changes in performance that result from it* is an ongoing process that is a critical part of the regularly scheduled review of a student's progress in all areas. The Individuals with Disabilities Education Act (IDEA) requires that the progress of students with an Individualized Education Program (IEP) is reviewed at least as frequently as that of all other students; for example, reviews may correspond to the report card schedule for all students. During each progress review, IEP team members *analyze data about the student's progress and performance*. If analysis of the data indicates that adjustments are needed, *changes are made* in the nature, schedule, or amount of AT services provided to the student.

When evaluating the effectiveness of a student's AT use, the team asks questions about the quality, frequency, and impact the AT devices and services have had in advancing the student's progress toward meeting goals. A consistent data collection and review process helps the team determine the effectiveness of AT use. When they analyze student performance, the team members can make necessary adjustments and avoid errors such as:

- assuming the student has skills that are not yet developed,

- assuming the student does not have skills that are already mastered, or

- assuming the device is the problem when it is not.

Any of these erroneous assumptions can lead to premature abandonment of the AT.

To be most effective, creating a timeline for evaluating the effectiveness of AT implementation occurs along with the development of the implementation plan. Initial steps for creating a relevant plan to evaluate the effectiveness of AT use include

- convening people who will be involved in supporting the student's use of AT;

- referring to the goal(s) for which the AT is required so that the student can progress toward mastery of the goal(s);

- aligning the implementation plan with the evaluation plan so it can provide evidence to show what is working and should be continued, as well as what is not working and should be changed in some way; and

- identifying a shared expectation for the use of the AT and agreeing on the criteria to be used to determine the extent to which the expectation has been met.

The Planning Process for Evaluating the Effectiveness of Assistive Technology

A well-crafted evaluation plan that is closely aligned with implementation enables team members to determine the effectiveness of the AT and to make changes when needed. The following steps are based on the "Plan for Evaluation of Effectiveness of AT Use" included at the end of this chapter.

Using Present Levels of Performance as Baseline Data

The present levels of academic achievement and functional performance identified in the IEP and the implementation plan serve as the baseline for data collection. Baseline data provide information about the student's initial performance **related to the goal(s)** and about the specific tasks that are critical to moving toward mastery of the goal(s). Although present levels are identified during the development of the IEP, more specific and quantifiable information is added when planning for evaluation of the AT use.

Establishing Changes in Performance That are Expected as a Result of Implementation

When the implementation plan was developed, the team agreed on the changes that would be desirable, realistic, and observable as the student used the AT to progress toward **mastery of one or more goals**. In the next step, the team clearly defines and agrees on where and how changes will be measured to demonstrate the student's progress **across environments** during naturally occurring and structured activities for which the AT is intended to be used (e.g., "Student will be able to _____").

Based on the desired changes in performance that were identified, the team determines the **quantitative and qualitative measurements** that will be documented. Depending upon the goal and the expected change, the team considers whether the desired change is an increase or a decrease in some aspect of performance. Examples of aspects that may be identified for change may be one or more of the following: spontaneity, frequency, duration, accuracy, productivity, level of participation, independence, quality of work, and satisfaction.

Issues the team discusses will vary according to the purpose of the AT and the aspects of changes in student performance that need to be measured. Examples that may be helpful to teams include the following:

- If the student is expected to express themselves more quickly when using AT, what data will be needed to demonstrate the extent to which that has occurred?

- If, when using AT and accessible formats of materials, the student is expected to read for a longer period of time before becoming fatigued, what data will be needed to demonstrate that this has occurred?

- If AT is expected to enable the student to use more grade-level vocabulary in written compositions, what data will be needed to demonstrate the extent to which that has occurred?

Determining Obstacles That May Inhibit Success

When the implementation plan was made, the team identified internal and external barriers that might inhibit the student's success (e.g., absenteeism, lack of needed supports, health issues, unavailability of the technology, lack of knowledge about the task). When developing the evaluation plan, the team determines where and how to collect data that would demonstrate the extent to which those barriers did or did not occur. These data provide a means for **analyzing student achievement** and **the impact of any barriers to progress that occurred**. Examples of questions the team might ask about obstacles include the following:

- Does the student understand how to do the tasks for which the AT is provided (e.g., write an essay, participate in a discussion, prepare by reading an assigned chapter)?

- Has the student had sufficient instruction in how to use the AT for the expected tasks?

- Do team members provide opportunities for the student to use the AT when and where it is intended to be used?

- Are there other factors that prohibit the student from having sufficient opportunities to gain proficiency in both the tasks and technology use (e.g., absences, schedule changes, failure of team members to provide opportunities)?

- Has adequate training for families and educators been provided?

If these or any other barriers occur and are not captured in data analysis, they could lead to incorrect assumptions about the effectiveness of use of the AT. Collecting data on the use of AT without the student having adequate training or appropriate educational instruction may lead a team to believe the AT was not useful when, in fact, the student needed additional training and instruction. For example, providing a writing tool that enables a student to write an essay does not mean that the student knows how to write an essay.

After potential barriers are identified, the team determines how they will document the extent to which the barriers did or did not occur and the extent to which needed supports were provided. These data provide valuable information that teams can use to reduce barriers when possible. Examples of questions for the team to explore may include the following:

- What data will be collected to document the internal and external factors that could negatively impact the student's progress? For example, if attendance has been identified as a potential barrier, an attendance record already in place can be used to determine whether absences were a factor.

- How often will data on potential barriers be collected and reported and by whom and to whom? Do the student and the team members have all the training and supports they need?

- How will data on external factors be reported and by whom and to whom?

Determining the Methods to Be Used to Collect the Data

The choice of how and when to collect data is based on the type of change expected and the evidence that can best reflect that change. Once the team has defined what the student needs to be able to do and the changes that are expected, they can design a plan to collect the **quantitative and qualitative data** that demonstrate the identified change.

Four primary methods of collecting data about AT use were identified by Reed, Bowser, and Korsten (2002) in *How Do You Know It? How Can You Show It?*:

1. Interviewing the student, their family, staff members, and allies
2. Reviewing finished products the student created using AT
3. Observing the student working on the task(s) for which the AT is needed
4. Recording the student doing the task with and without the AT

When determining the conditions that can increase the data's reliability, consider the following factors:

- *Locations of data collection:* When AT is used across environments, collecting effectiveness data in each place provides a clearer picture of the student's overall progress.

- *Frequency of data collection:* Frequent data collection on an agreed-upon schedule increases the chances of seeing patterns and trends in the data, which can lead to more accurate decisions.

- *Impact of uncontrollable or unexpected factors:* If data are collected on an infrequent basis, the impact of uncontrollable factors may not be recognized and may seriously impact decisions.

- *Consistency of data collection:* When identified data collection methods and tools are used by all as intended, data can be combined more easily to determine if the expected changes are occurring.

- *Ease of data collection:* The easier it is to collect the data, the more likely it is the data needed will be collected.

- *Observer reliability:* Reliability is increased when everyone is clear about what the observable change should look like and all agree about what they are trying to observe and measure.

Next Steps

A comprehensive data collection plan ensures that the roles, responsibilities, and timelines for collection and analysis of data are clearly defined and understood by all involved. It also includes an indication of when changes to the implementation plan will be made if the data indicate the need for change. Questions that will help the team feel confident about the quality of the plan may include the following:

- Is the evaluation of effectiveness plan aligned with the implementation plan?
- Have baselines related to targeted goals and tasks been established?
- Are the aspects of change identified and agreed upon?
- Have ways to measure internal and external barriers been identified?
- Have data collection tasks in each environment where the AT is to be used been identified and assigned?
- Are the types of data that will demonstrate change and the procedures for collecting those data determined and understood by all across the entire plan?
- Does the plan include a timeline for collection and review of data (e.g., every time the task occurs, weekly, daily, when a barrier occurs)?
- Has a person been identified to monitor the plan to ensure that all aspects of the plan are followed?
- Has a strategy been identified to ensure that changes are made in the implementation when the analysis of evaluation data indicates that change is needed?

A well-designed plan for evaluating the effectiveness of AT implementation enables all involved to clearly understand the goal(s) of AT use and the expected changes in the student's performance. It also includes the types of data that will show the extent to which expected—and unexpected—change has or has not occurred, any barriers encountered, and supports provided. An effective plan also requires team members to have a deep understanding of the "what, where, when, and by whom" of data collection and a collective commitment to fulfill their individual roles in the plan.

Ideally, the evaluation of effectiveness plan and the implementation plan are put in place simultaneously. When an evaluation plan is carefully crafted, the details align closely with the activities of the implementation plan. The strategies in the evaluation of effectiveness plan need to be specific and robust enough to determine if the current educational program and AT services enable the student to make progress toward identified goals. If not, data can be used to decide what changes need to be made to increase the student's achievement.

Resources

The following resources support the content of this chapter.

Forms

- ***Plan for Evaluation of Effectiveness of AT Use*** (*www.qiat.org*)

    This form is designed to help a team identify the steps in evaluating the effectiveness of an individual student's AT use and make a plan for completing the evaluation.

- ***Activity-Based Implementation and Evaluation Plan Summary*** (*http://www.joyzabala.com/uploads/Zabala_SETT_Scaffold_Implementation.pdf*)

    This is one of several forms in a sequence that assists IEP teams with planning for implementation of a student's AT use. The plan aligns evaluation of effectiveness with implementation activities.

Publications

- Reed, P., Bowser, G., & Korsten, J. (2002). *How do you know it? How can you show it?* (*https://educationtechpoints.org/knowledge-base/resources-for-periodic-review*)

    This manual discusses strategies for data collection and analysis. The link above takes you to a free copy to download.

- Korsten, J., Foss, T., & Berry, L. (2007). *Every move counts, clicks and chats: EMC3*. Lee's Summit, MO: EMC Communications (*www.everymovecounts.net*).

    This comprehensive manual addresses the development of communication skills for students with complex communication needs. It includes a significant focus on the use of data to analyze student needs and initial communication efforts and to use that data to evaluate the student's progress and make needed adjustments to the program.

Plan for Evaluation of Effectiveness of AT Use

Student's Name: _____

Student ID: _____ Grade: _____ Date: _____

School Agency: _____

Team members present: _____

The intent of this document is to guide planning about how the use of assistive technology will be evaluated. Completion of this document will help the team to create a shared vision of the process for data collection.

IEP Goal: _____

Step 1: What is the present level of performance (baseline data) on this goal?	Describe:
Step 2: What changes are expected as a result of implementation? (e.g., Student will be able to _____.)	Describe:
Step 3: What aspects will change? ❑ Quality ❑ Independence ❑ Quantity/productivity ❑ Spontaneity ❑ Frequency ❑ Duration ❑ Participation ❑ _____	Describe:
Step 4: What obstacles may inhibit success? ❑ Physical access ❑ Skill ❑ Opportunity ❑ Attitude ❑ Instruction/practice ❑ Medical ❑ Student preference ❑ _____	Describe:
Step 5: How will the occurrence of obstacles be reflected in the data?	Describe:

44 ■ THE QIAT COMPANION

Step 6: What format will be used to collect the data?

❏ Report (self, other) ❏ Audio/video recording

❏ Work samples ❏ _____

❏ Observation

Describe:

Step 7: What is the data collection plan?

Environment(s): _____

Activity: _____

Frequency: _____

Person(s) responsible: _____

    Data Collection _____

    Data Analysis _____

    Changes in Response to Analysis _____

Review date(s): _____

CHAPTER 6

Quality Indicators for Assistive Technology Transition

1. *Transition plans address the AT needs* of the student, including roles and training needs of team members, subsequent steps in AT use, and follow-up after transition takes place.

2. Transition planning empowers the student using AT to participate in the transition planning at a level appropriate to age and ability.

3. Advocacy related to AT use is recognized as critical and planned for by the teams involved in transition.

4. AT requirements in the receiving environment are identified during the transition planning process.

5. Transition planning for students using AT proceeds according to an individualized timeline.

6. Transition plans address specific equipment, training, and funding issues, such as transfer or acquisition of AT, manuals, and support documents.

Ensuring Quality in Assistive Technology Transition

There are multiple, naturally occurring transition points for students with disabilities. Some are shaped by policy, such as the transition from Part C to Part B, or the transition from Part B to postsecondary life. Some transitions occur for students as they move from classroom to classroom, grade to grade, or district to district. Transitions within education agencies may range from providing early intervention for infants and toddlers with disabilities to helping secondary students make the transition to postsecondary, community, or work settings. Effective planning is needed for each transition to ensure that the student's assistive technology (AT) use continues uninterrupted in each new setting. Some student needs are consistent across all environments.

AT transition planning involves people from different classrooms, programs, buildings, and/or agencies working together to ensure continuity. The sending and receiving settings both play an important role in planning to ensure that students who use AT have access to the devices and supports they need in order to continue to be as independent and productive as possible. Transition planning for students preparing to graduate from high school includes development of self-determination skills and a comprehensive approach to how the student will receive the accessible materials, AT, and supports they will need in the new setting.

The AT Transition Planning Process

Collaboration and planning between current and future settings helps to ensure that a student transitioning to new settings will continue to have access to AT devices and services needed to build upon and increase the progress they are making the current settings. Each aspect of the AT Transition Planning Process is important to successful transitions whether they be from school to post school or just from one school or class to another.

Addressing the Student's AT Needs

Effective transition plans for students who use AT specifically **address the student's needs for AT devices** and how the student's use of AT will be transferred from one setting to another. The need for ongoing support services after the transition occurs is an essential element of the planning. The plan also addresses the roles and training needs of educators, and ongoing accountability for implementing the plan. It is also critical to plan for capacity in the new setting: what devices need to be available, the roles of the team members supporting the transitioning student, and staff members' ability to implement the needed devices and supports. Staff from both the sending and receiving environments, the student, and family will all benefit from meeting to plan for the student's access to the appropriate AT and access to support services. The resulting transition plan will ensure that necessary supports are assigned and that there is accountability in providing those supports.

Empowering the Student

Planning for transition gives **students the opportunity to be empowered** and to partner in planning for the new setting. This practice is especially important for secondary students for developing self-determination and making a successful transition. It is critical that students learn to the extent possible the skills of self-determination, so they can express their own needs and expectations in a new setting. Self-determination skills include

- choice-making,
- decision-making,
- problem-solving,
- goal-setting and attainment,
- self-regulation and self-management, and
- Self-advocacy and leadership.

The earlier these skills are taught, the more successful students can be in making decisions about their transition needs as they relate to AT in their current and future environments.

Including Advocacy

Effective advocacy for the use of AT is critical to the student's success in the new environment. Many voices are needed in the transition planning so that all the student's needs related to AT use and support are considered. These voices include the student making the transition and family members, as well as stakeholders in the sending and receiving environments. As the team and the student focus on the new tasks and environments the student will experience, they will examine the opportunities to use AT in the new setting and advocate for its use.

Identifying Requirements in the New Setting

The transition process includes opportunities for communication between settings and agencies; visits by the students, families, and teachers; and planning meetings that include all needed team members. The team, which includes the student and family members, will need to gather information about the **requirements and the tasks that will be part of the new environment.** The sending and receiving teams collaborate and share information on what has worked, why it has worked, and the supports that have been critical to the student's achievement. Planning addresses what AT is needed, the requirements for implementation, and access to support services.

Addressing Equipment, Training, and Funding Issues

Issues such as **equipment** (e.g., hardware, software, manuals, cords), **training, and funding will need to be addressed**. The Individualized Education Program (IEP) team will want to research issues related to the new environment before the transition occurs so the student will have the supports and resources they need in place from the first day in the new setting. Multiple team members will take part, including those representing the sending and receiving sites, the student, family, related service providers, and outside agencies, as appropriate. Questions to explore about these issues include the following:

- What tasks need to be completed?
- What supports will be needed and how will they be provided?
- What AT devices are used in the new setting?
- Will the AT the student has used in the sending environment work in the new environment?
- Will the AT be transferred? If it is transferred, will it have any accompanying documentation (e.g., user guides, repair history)?
- If it is not transferred, how will the appropriate AT be identified and procured?
- What training will be needed in the new setting for both the student and staff?
- Are staff in the new setting prepared to support the student's use of AT and invested in doing so?
- What funding is available?
- Who will provide services or troubleshoot?

Planning Proceeds According to Individualized Timelines

When teams plan for transitions, they will **consider timelines for that transition that are based on the student's unique needs.** The team should focus on the distinct tasks, challenges, opportunities, and expectations in the new environment. It is critical to examine whether the AT the student has used successfully in the current setting will meet the changing tasks and requirements of the new environment.

When students are transitioning from Part B services due to graduation or aging out to postsecondary settings, the Individuals with Disabilities Education Act (IDEA) specifically defines the transition services that are to be in place.

Transition Services.

(A) Transition services means a coordinated set of activities for a child with a disability that—

Is designed to be within a results-oriented process, that is focused on improving the academic and functional achievement of the child with a disability to facilitate the child's movement from school to post-school activities, including postsecondary education, vocational education, integrated employment (including supported employment), continuing and adult education, adult services, independent living, or community participation;

Is based on the individual child's needs, taking into account the child's strengths, preferences, and interests; and includes—

> (i) Instruction;
>
> (ii) Related services;
>
> (iii) Community experiences;
>
> (iv) The development of employment and other post-school adult living objectives; and
>
> (v) If appropriate, acquisition of daily living skills and provision of a functional vocational evaluation.
>
> (B) Transition services for children with disabilities may be special education, if provided as specially designed instruction, or a related service, if required to assist a child with a disability to benefit from special education.

(34 C.F.R.§300.43)

IDEA states that the services should begin no later than with the first IEP to be in effect when the child turns 16, or younger if determined appropriate by the IEP team or by state or local policy.

Definition of Individualized Education Program.

> (b) Transition services. Beginning not later than the first IEP to be in effect when the child turns 16, or younger if determined appropriate by the IEP Team, and updated annually, thereafter, the IEP must include—
>
> Appropriate measurable postsecondary goals based upon age appropriate transition assessments related to training, education, employment, and, where appropriate, independent living skills; and
>
> The transition services (including courses of study) needed to assist the child in reaching those goals.

(34 C.F.R. §300.320)

Next Steps

To promote clarity and consistency in the transition process, schools and programs develop a process and an accompanying form to ensure that all elements of the process are addressed across teams. The "QIAT Transition Planning Worksheet for AT Users" included at the end of this chapter is one example. This worksheet addresses issues that are relevant in all transitions, as well as the "Coordinated Plan for Transition Activities," which IDEA requires when a student transitions to a postsecondary setting.

Transition plans document who the primary contact for AT services will be in the new setting. Sometimes this will be an educator, although adult services need to be identified for students who leave the K–12 system. The plans also identify the range of services that will be needed so those can be matched with appropriate service providers. Transition planning incorporates documenting the transfer of AT devices, as well as outlining the steps to facilitate a smooth transition, including collaboration between staff at the sending and receiving agencies and visits by the student to the new setting.

Higher education does not have to comply with the IDEA requirement to identify students who might need services. Postsecondary students have the responsibility to disclose their own special needs, thus their self-determination skills and the support of advocates are essential for effective follow-through and the implementation of any transition plan.

Resources

The following resources support the content of this chapter.

Guide

- ***A Transition Guide to Postsecondary Education and Employment for Students and Youth with Disabilities*** (*https://www2.ed.gov/about/offices/list/osers/transition/products/postsecondary-transition-guide-may-2017.pdf*).

    This transition guide by the U.S. Department of Education, Office of Special Education and Rehabilitative Services, addresses a broad range of topics that facilitate a seamless transition from school to post-school activities, including the planning process and legal requirements.

Training

- ***AT Transitions, Assistive Technology Internet Modules (ATIM)*** (*https://atinternetmodules.org*)

    Developed by the Ohio Center for Autism and Low Incidence (OCALI) and partners, this module provides information for IEP teams as they plan transitions that include AT.

- ***Transition Module: Supporting Transitions of Assistive Technology Users*** (*http://www.texasat.net/training-modules/transition-module*).

    The content, processes, and strategies presented in this module created by the Texas Assistive Technology Network (TATN) are appropriate for transitions of AT users at any age and are not specific to Texas.

Website

- ***QIAT in Post Secondary Education*** (*http://qiat-ps.org*)

    The tools created by the QIAT-PS project include a set of indicators for post-secondary institutions, as well as for individual students in post-secondary education settings. They offer a coordinated framework to support the transition process to post-secondary educational environments.

Transition Planning Worksheet for AT Users

Student: _____ Age: _____

Indicate Transition:

❏ Early Childhood to School ❏ Program to Program

❏ School to School ❏ School to Post-secondary

Persons completing this worksheet: _____

NAME OF PROGRAM AND/OR SCHOOL	
Current Placement & Services:	Future Setting & Services:

NAME THE PRIMARY POINT OF CONTACT (E.G., SERVICES COORDINATOR, SUPERVISOR) WITH CONTACT INFORMATION (E.G., PHONE NUMBER, EMAIL ADDRESS).

Current Setting:	Future Setting:

SERVICES NEEDED IN FUTURE SETTING (E.G., OT, PT, SPEECH/LANGUAGE, TRANSPORTATION, MEDICAL)	PERSON	DATE

QUALITY INDICATORS FOR ASSISTIVE TECHNOLOGY TRANSITION ■ 53

(continued)

GENERAL TRANSITION TASKS TO BE COMPLETED	PERSON	DATE
▪ Staff members from current setting observe in future setting		
▪ Student/family visit future setting		
▪ Staff from both settings meet to plan		
▪ Arrange enrollment in needed non-school services (e.g., DD, VR)		
Other: _____		

DEVICE SPECIFIC TASKS TO BE COMPLETED NAME/TYPE OF AT USED: _____	PERSON	DATE
▪ Arrange transfer of technology including manuals, service records		
▪ Create artifacts to demonstrate current level of use and independence (e.g., video recording, work samples)		
▪ Identify any new technology that may be needed in future setting		
▪ Identify sources of funding for new technology		
▪ Identify person(s) to do troubleshooting in future setting		
Other: _____		

AT SKILLS TO INCREASE STUDENT INDEPENDENCE (TO BE INCLUDED IN IEP AS NECESSARY)
Device-specific use/operational skills: Knowing how to operate the technology
Functional Use Skills: Using AT to accomplish meaningful tasks across settings
Strategic Skills: Choosing the right tool for a specific task
Social Skills: Using technology effectively and appropriately around other people

**AT SKILLS TO INCREASE STUDENT SELF DETERMINATION
(TO BE INCLUDED IN IEP AS NECESSARY)**

Choice-making:

Decision-making:

Problem-solving:

Goal-setting/attainment:

Self-regulation/self-management:

Self-advocacy/leadership:

(continued)

TRANSITION TO POST-SECONDARY SETTINGS
COORDINATED PLAN FOR TRANSITION ACTIVITIES SUMMARY

Transition planning teams should consider how the student's current or future AT use will impact success in each of these transition areas.

❑ **Instruction**—Is instruction needed to prepare the student for new settings? Is the current AT appropriate? Will additional devices or services be needed for new settings?

❑ **Related Services**—Is there a need for additional related services to prepare the student for post-secondary life? Are the current related services supporting AT use needed in future settings? Who will provide these? How can the student/family connect with necessary services?

❑ **Community Experiences**—What opportunities need to be provided for the student to use AT in community experiences to prepare for post-secondary life, including socialization, recreation, banking, transportation, etc.?

❑ **Employment**—If AT will be used as part of the student's employability, what services and strategies need to be considered? What activities using AT are needed to develop work-related skills, including job seeking and retention skills, career exploration, and paid employment?

❑ **Post-school Adult Living**—What activities will be needed to prepare the student to use his AT in developing independence in adult living, including accessing medical services, registering to vote, accessing transportation, and paying rent and other bills?

❑ **Daily Living Skills**—What activities will be needed to prepare the student to use her AT in developing independence in daily living, such as cooking, dressing, shopping, maintaining health and hygiene, housekeeping, etc.?

❑ **Functional Vocational Evaluation**—How is the use of AT incorporated into the vocational evaluation? Do the evaluation results indicate a need for continued use of AT or the use of new AT?

CHAPTER 7

Quality Indicators for Administrative Support of Assistive Technology Services

1. The education agency has written procedural guidelines that ensure equitable access to assistive technology devices and services for students with disabilities, if required for a free appropriate, public education (FAPE).

2. The education agency broadly disseminates clearly defined procedures for accessing and providing assistive technology services and supports the implementation of those guidelines.

3. The education agency includes appropriate assistive technology responsibilities in written descriptions of job requirements for each position in which activities impact assistive technology services.

4. The education agency employs personnel with the competencies needed to support quality assistive technology services within their primary areas of responsibility at all levels of the organization.

5. The education agency includes assistive technology in the technology planning and budgeting process.

6. The education agency provides access to on-going learning opportunities about assistive technology for staff, family, and students.

7. The education agency uses a systematic process to evaluate all components of the agency-wide assistive technology program.

Ensuring Quality AT Services

Administrative support is essential to developing and sustaining quality assistive technology (AT) services. Administrators have influence over multiple aspects of an agency. They can be change leaders, cheerleaders, supporters, motivators, and resource providers. They value and work with others to increase the quality and consistency of educational opportunities for all students across programs, buildings, and at all educational levels. The Quality Indicators for Administrative Support of Assistive Technology Services help administrators ensure that AT devices and consistent, equitable, and effective AT services are provided to all students who need them.

Developing Written Procedural Guidelines

Developing **written procedural guidelines** is one of the most effective ways to ensure consistent and quality AT services across an agency, regardless of a student's disability, educational placement, geographic location, or economic status. Guidelines for AT services address common procedures that are part of the educational process for any student with a disability. They often include steps of the process related to the following:

- Considering the student's need for AT during the Individualized Education Program (IEP) meeting
- Referring a student for AT evaluation
- Evaluating a student's need for AT
- Including AT in the IEP in effective, meaningful ways
- Using school-owned AT in other settings (e.g., home, community)
- Planning implementation of the student's use of AT
- Evaluating the effectiveness of the AT use
- Planning transitions for a student who uses AT

Creating guidelines related to other issues that may occur is also helpful. These might include:

- Addressing recommendations for AT from a contracted assessment
- Seeking funding for AT from an outside source
- Taking actions if an AT device is lost, stolen, or damaged
- Providing AT services in charter and private schools
- Transferring technology from one agency to another

Disseminating Procedural Guidelines

For written guidelines to be effective, **broad dissemination** is essential. Service providers from across the agency, as well as students' families, need to be aware that the agency has AT operating guidelines and know where to find them. Dissemination efforts are more successful when multiple distribution methods are used. Providing both print and online versions ensures that educators and families will be able to quickly locate and use the guidelines when needed. Guidelines are more likely to be useful if administrators clearly convey the expectation that they will be followed and periodically remind IEP team members about the guideline contents and location.

Building the AT Competence of Educators, Students, and Families

Delivering quality AT services requires that people with varied knowledge, skills, and backgrounds have the competencies needed to fulfill their roles and the ability to collaborate effectively. When administrators identify the AT competencies needed by staff, students, and families, include staff competencies listed in job descriptions, and provide support for ongoing learning opportunities, the likelihood that AT services will be aligned, equitable, and effective increases significantly.

Identifying Competencies Needed to Support AT

Everyone who works directly with students with disabilities, including general educators, needs basic information about AT, such as the following:

- What IDEA says about AT devices and services
- Factors that indicate a student might need AT
- Actions required for effective staff, student, and family participation in AT consideration during the IEP meeting
- Who to contact within the school building or district to find out more about AT
- The agency's process for making a referral for AT devices and services when needed
- Strategies to determine whether the AT, when provided and used in the way intended, is making a difference in the student's participation and achievement

In addition to this basic knowledge, everyone on the team, including the student, family members, and school staff (e.g., administrators, teachers, therapists, instructional assistants, technology specialists or integrators), may need specialized skills that relate in some way to the selection and use of AT. Not all need the same competencies; which ones each team member need will depend on their roles and responsibilities. For more information about competencies, see the resource section of this chapter.

Including AT in Job Descriptions

To ensure that the agency employs **personnel with the competencies needed** to support quality AT services in their primary areas of responsibility, staff recruitment, support, and retention are critically important. The specific skills needed to meet students' needs are first communicated through job announcements and in ***written job descriptions,*** and later through staff observations and evaluations. For example, a teacher's job description may include responsibilities related to technology (e.g., identifying and selecting instructional resources to meet students' varying learning needs, using relevant technology to support instruction, monitoring students' use of technology for educational achievement). AT fits well into these typical requirements and can be made more explicit in all job descriptions by adding the words "including AT" to one or more of them. Administrators may also want to ask job applicants questions specifically related to a teacher's ability to plan for and provide access to a student's AT while engaged in other daily activities.

Including AT Competencies in Staff Evaluations

One of the most powerful ways to prompt the development of AT competencies is to include them in staff evaluations. Administrators who include AT expectations in staff evaluations can use the results to make decisions about professional development needs.

Providing Ongoing Learning Opportunities

AT services are more likely to be aligned, equitable, and effective when individuals are offered ongoing learning opportunities. Administrators encourage growth in providing quality AT services when they consider the information, knowledge, and skills their staff and students' families need, and when they support participation in ongoing learning opportunities that address those needs. Well-prepared team members who have varied knowledge, skills, and backgrounds can move toward a shared vision by contributing ideas, information, and direction based on their unique perspectives. (See Chapter 8, "Quality Indicators for Professional Development and Training in Assistive Technology," for additional information.)

Including AT in Program Management

Program management is an important administrative task. Ensuring that AT services are high-quality, relevant and equitable involves collaborative planning and budgeting across general and special education and periodic, comprehensive evaluation of all phases of AT service delivery.

Planning and Budgeting Process

Administrators in both general education and special education can work together to ensure that AT is included in the agency-wide technology ***planning and budgeting*** *process*. When the agency acquires universally designed technology for all students, it can be used by students across a broad range of abilities and needs, either directly (without AT) or through interoperability with AT. Usability and accessibility increase when a technology includes multiple options that can be turned off and on, depending on individual preferences or needs.

Evaluating the AT Program

A periodic review of the processes and outcomes of the AT program provides information that can be used to further develop and improve the agency's AT services. The quality indicators in the eight areas included in Quality Indicators for Assistive Technology (QIAT) can be used to identify components of the program that should be evaluated. The QIAT Self-Evaluation Matrices, included in Appendix B, can be used to determine areas of strength and those needing improvement. Two of several important features of a high-quality AT program evaluation are (1) collecting data related to each specific component of the AT program, and (2) soliciting input from people who have been involved in any part of the AT program, including teachers, therapists, students, families, and others.

As a result of the program evaluation, administrators and others can analyze the data and ask themselves the following:

- What components are working well?
- What components are priorities for improvement?
- What actions will be taken in response to the results of the program evaluation?

Next Steps

Administrators striving to improve administrative services in their program or agency can do so by attending sessions at administrators' conferences, reading articles in their professional journals, and seeking out opportunities to work with colleagues within their school district. The "QIAT Administrators' Planner for Effective Technology Supervision and Leadership," included at the end of this chapter, suggests specific actions administrators can take to support all aspects of providing high-quality AT services. Additional resources are provided below for further study.

Resources

The following resources support the content of this chapter.

Guides

- ***Connecticut Assistive Technology Competencies*** (*https://portal.ct.gov/SDE /Publications/Assistive-Technology-Guidelines-Section-1-For-Ages-3-21 /Assistive-Technology-Service-Providers-Competency*).

Guidance developed by the Connecticut Department of Education includes AT competencies for both AT professionals and IEP team members. These competencies help administrators know what to look for in hiring, supervising, and evaluating staff, and for providing learning opportunities.

- **Florida Assistive Technology Competencies** (*https://at-udl.com/library/wp-content/uploads/2014/10/AT-Competencies-April-2016-1.pdf*).

    This guidance developed by the Florida Department of Education includes AT competencies for both AT professionals and IEP team members. These competencies help administrators know what to look for in hiring, supervising, and evaluating staff, and for providing learning opportunities.

References

- Bowser, G., & Reed, P. (2012). *Education tech points: A framework for assistive technology*. Winchester, OR: Coalition for Assistive Technology in Oregon.

    Education Tech Points is a commercial product that offers information and suggestions for AT actions at each stage of the special education process. The manual includes sample forms and resources schools can use to develop a comprehensive AT process that is equitable for all students.

- Bowser, G., & Reed, P. (2018). *Leading the way to excellence in AT services: A guide for school administrators*. Wakefield, MA: CAST Professional Publishing.

    This resource examines four aspects of school administration and explains the legal, ethical, and practical reasons for providing high-quality AT to students who need it.

Training

- **AT for Administrators, Assistive Technology Internet Modules** (*https://atinternetmodules.org*).

    This administrative module is one of many developed by the Ohio Center for Autism and Low Incidence (OCALI) and partners.

- **Leadership: Making Quality Assistive Technology Services Sustainable** (*http://www.texasat.net/training-modules/leadership-module*).

    This module created by the Texas Assistive Technology Network discusses the roles administrators, managers, and leaders play in ensuring that quality AT services are provided in a sustainable model.

Administrators' Planner for Effective Technology Supervision and Leadership

Principals and administrative leaders are powerful change agents. Research shows that perceived pressure from principals and other administrators to use technology is one of the most powerful factors in increasing technology use for teaching and learning (O'Dwyer, Russell, & Bebell, 2004). This planner can be used to support and guide administrators in their work as they identify effective technology use, including assistive technology (AT), and mentor teachers and staff. Suggestions for use include staff discussion of service quality, goal-setting, supervision, continuous improvement efforts, monitoring, and progress assessment.

EFFECTIVE TECHNOLOGY LEADERSHIP FOR PRINCIPALS AND OTHER ADMINISTRATORS	YES	NO
Principals and teachers have clearly defined, shared expectations of the importance of implementing technology, including AT, in teaching and learning.		
Administrators' expectations for technology use including AT are communicated throughout the school year in a variety of ways.		
Administrators ensure that teachers have equitable access to current technologies, software, appropriate technical support, and the Internet.		
Reward structures (e.g., recognition, opportunities to share, credits toward salary advancement) are in place to support technology in teaching and learning.		
Administrators ensure that principals and teachers know how to access resources to support students who need additional technology assistance.		
EFFECTIVE TECHNOLOGY PRACTICE FOR TEACHERS		
Teachers are skilled in the use of technology for preparing and delivering instruction.		
Teachers access professional development opportunities to support technology use in teaching and learning.		
Teachers ensure that technology is available and operational and seek technical assistance in a timely manner.		
Teachers utilize innovative ideas for using technology resources to support standards-based instruction.		
Teachers facilitate appropriate student use of technology-based resources using a variety of applications.		
Teachers regularly measure the effectiveness of technology for learning.		
Teachers proactively incorporate technology into teaching and learning activities to support diverse learners.		
Teachers ensure that students have the opportunity to use the technology, including assistive technology, written into their IEPs.		
Teachers routinely include specific evidence about technology use when reporting student progress to parents.		

(continued)

EFFECTIVE TECHNOLOGY USE BY STUDENTS	YES	NO
Students regularly use technology, including assistive technology, as required to participate in learning activities, complete assignments, and interact with peers.		
Students who experience difficulty with reading use technology to access information, acquire knowledge, and demonstrate skills.		
Students who experience difficulty with writing use technology to demonstrate knowledge and skills.		
Students who experience difficulty with physical or sensory access to classroom materials use technology to access the curriculum and demonstrate knowledge and skills.		
Students who experience difficulty with math use technology to access information, acquire knowledge, and demonstrate skills.		
Students who experience difficulty with oral communication use technology to support communication efforts.		

Encouraging Effective Technology Use in Schools

One of an administrator's responsibilities is to manage the technology that is currently used. However, it is important to point out that when considering AT for an individual student, a wide range of options should be considered in addition to what is available in the district.

A school leader can encourage appropriate and effective use of technology by:

1. Involving staff in the creation of a school-wide technology plan that includes AT
2. Leading staff in becoming familiar with the educational and assistive technology available at their school
3. Encouraging staff to become familiar with resources to support technology use at school, district, and statewide levels
4. Periodically assessing the technology training needs of staff at your school
5. Planning professional development about teaching with technology
6. Using Universal Design for Learning strategies to support the needs of diverse learners

    - Advocating for technology that supports accessibility for diverse learners.
    - Promoting the use of technology-based learning activities in line with curriculum objectives

7. Publically recognizing effective technology use (e.g., highlight effective practices at staff meetings, bulletin board postings, peer sharing, and newsletter articles)

8. Creating a database of all assistive and educational technology used in the building in order to:

    - Obtain information about what the district has committed to provide to meet individual student needs
    - Monitor building-wide usage
    - Plan for future needs

9. Monitoring AT consideration at IEP meetings to ensure that AT is considered for every student receiving special education

10. Making a master list of assistive technology included in each IEP. Prior to a teacher observation, check the master list to determine which students should have technology available and operational in that class

11. Ensuring timely technical support and repairs to support continuous student achievement

References for Administrators' Planner

O'Dwyer, L. M., Russell, M. & Bebell, D. J. (2004, September 14). Identifying teacher, school and district characteristics associated with elementary teachers' use of technology: A multilevel perspective. *Education Policy Analysis Archives,* 12(48).

International Society for Technology in Education (2003). *National educational technology standards for teachers*. Eugene, OR: Author. Retrieved from *http://www.iste.org/standards/ISTE-standards/standards-for-teachers*.

CHAPTER 8

Quality Indicators for Professional Development and Training in Assistive Technology

1. Comprehensive assistive technology professional development and training *support the understanding that assistive technology devices and services enable students to accomplish IEP goals and objectives and make progress in the general curriculum.*

2. The education agency has an AT professional development and training *plan that identifies the audiences, the purposes, the activities, the expected results, evaluation measures and funding* for assistive technology professional development and training.

3. The content of comprehensive AT professional development and training *addresses all aspects of the selection, acquisition and use of assistive technology.*

4. AT professional development and training address and are *aligned with other local, state and national professional development initiatives.*

5. Assistive technology professional development and training *include ongoing learning opportunities that utilize local, regional, and/or national resources.*

6. Professional development and training in assistive technology follow *research-based models for adult learning* that include multiple formats and are delivered at multiple skill levels.

7. The effectiveness of assistive technology professional development and training is *evaluated by measuring changes in practice that result in improved student performance.*

Ensuring Quality Professional Development in Assistive Technology

Professional development is essential for building educators' and families' assistive technology (AT) knowledge and skills and for improving and sustaining quality services. The most effective AT professional development efforts arise out of an ongoing, well-defined, comprehensive plan. A plan for AT professional development supports the understanding that the purpose of *AT devices and services is to enable students to accomplish their individualized education program (IEP) goals and objectives and make progress in the general curriculum.* This understanding helps the planning team focus on professional development that will be meaningful to participants because it aligns with student needs and the provision of a free appropriate public education (FAPE).

Professional Development Planning Process

The effective selection and use of assistive technology devices and the provision of high-quality assistive technology services is complex. Educators and families require ongoing learning opportunities to build the capacities needed to fulfill their roles in supporting students who require AT devices and services. Each aspect of the Professional Development and Planning Process helps to ensure that needed training and support are available when and where needed.

Developing a Comprehensive Plan

Designing and implementing a comprehensive AT professional development plan includes clearly *identifying the audiences, purposes, activities, expected results, evaluation measures, and funding.* Each learning opportunity within the plan is developed with a specific purpose in mind so that identified needs are addressed and an intended outcome is achieved.

Determining the Content of Training Activities

Having a clear vision of the expected outcomes of AT professional development requires those providing the training to understand what quality AT services are and how to help others become skilled in the development and delivery of those services. AT professional development addresses *all aspects of the selection, acquisition, and use of AT.* Comprehensive planning for learning opportunities covers a wide range of topics, including

- legal issues,
- collaborative processes,
- continuums of AT devices and services,
- implementation strategies,
- locating and obtaining resources,

- action planning, and
- data collection and analysis.

Addressing Different Roles and Responsibilities

A comprehensive AT professional development plan enables individuals at all levels of the organization to develop and maintain their ability to provide high-quality AT services. The plan would include activities that address the AT roles and responsibilities of general education and special education teachers, related services personnel, support personnel, administrators, AT specialists, students' families, and others. Effective learning opportunities are offered in formats and at times that meet the needs of these adult learners. While a range of professional development activities can be offered, the intended outcome of all activities is to ensure that everyone has the knowledge and skills needed to provide sustained, high-quality AT services that result in increased student participation, achievement, and outcomes.

Aligning Content with Other Local, State, and National Initiatives

Some aspects of AT training are specifically related to the selection and use of AT (e.g., factors to consider when selecting an AT device, strategies for supporting the use of AT devices, models of AT service delivery). However, the relevance of AT training is most effectively demonstrated when it is aligned with ***other local, state, and national professional development*** related to educational improvement (e.g., strategies for improvement in literacy or other areas, student variability, instructional design, family voice). When AT training is integrated into other adult learning opportunities, it can be shown to be a way to broaden the impact of the work by demonstrating how students with disabilities can use AT to increase, improve, or maintain their participation and build skills on the topics addressed.

Using a Variety of Sources for Learning Opportunities

An effective AT professional development plan includes ***ongoing learning opportunities that utilize local, regional, and/or national resources.*** At the local level, AT can be infused into a district in-service plan as part of staff development days or as targeted opportunities. However, an ongoing, comprehensive plan also includes learning opportunities offered outside of the organization. To ensure that all have a means to participate, professional development is offered in a variety of ways, including face-to-face, online, digital, and print-based learning opportunities. In addition to time-constrained presentations and webinars offered around the country, recordings, blogs, and other online resources can support "just in time" learning opportunities. In-person or online book-study groups or professional learning communities (PLCs) can be formed around the exploration and discussion of pertinent topics and resources.

Using Research-based Adult Learning Strategies

Effective AT learning opportunities for educators and families are provided in ways that incorporate ***research-based models for adult learning that are delivered in***

multiple formats and at multiple skill levels. Adults learn in different ways and have many competing responsibilities. If learning opportunities are offered in a variety of ways at multiple, appropriate skill levels and at flexible times, participation is likely to increase and the expected outcomes are more likely to be met. Participants' engagement increases when professional development is based on adult learning strategies, such as

- involving adults in finding meaning in what they are learning,
- immediately implementing what was learned, and
- establishing attainable learning goals.

Even when high-quality training has introduced new knowledge and skills, the application of that knowledge and the sustained use of those skills in everyday settings is not automatic. Coaching, mentoring, and other kinds of job-embedded and follow-up support have proven beneficial in supporting the integration of new knowledge and skills into daily practice. When adults receive structured feedback and encouragement through ongoing coaching and mentoring, they are more likely to change their practice and implement new strategies in the manner intended.

Evaluating AT Professional Development

Determining changes that take place as a result of participation in learning opportunities is an important aspect of AT professional development and training. Conducting evaluation activities (e.g., surveys, pre-/post-tests, initial reflections) before and immediately after a learning opportunity takes place can be a useful way to determine increased awareness, information, and satisfaction. However, **evaluation that measures change in practice,** such as the application of new knowledge, use of new skills when and where needed, and fidelity to and sustained use of these new abilities, requires different evaluation strategies. Evaluation that measures changes in practice is generally ongoing and can take on many forms, including the following:

- Matrices or rubrics
- Interaction with coaches and mentors
- Surveys conducted after a period of time
- Observation of implementation occurring
- Interviews
- Portfolios
- Video and/or audio recordings

These and other types of ongoing evaluation help adult learners reflect on the lessons learned and provide an opportunity to receive feedback and to plan for follow-up in areas where they need further support. This level of evaluation is also crucial for the developers and providers of learning opportunities, because it enables them to see the extent to which the professional development plan and activities are having the intended impact. It also provides them with data needed to determine what may need to be modified to ensure that changes in practice occur and what the impact of those changes has been on student performance.

Professional development providers can use the Quality Indicators for Assistive Technology and the Self-Evaluation Matrices, included in Appendix B, to identify areas of strength and determine opportunities for growth. Use of the matrices shows where practice needs improvement and what better practice could look like. Use of the matrices before and after the development and provision of a systemic professional development plan can indicate that change has taken place as a result of the learning opportunities—or that it has not.

Next Steps

A comprehensive AT professional development plan is needed to enable educators to provide effective, sustainable, high-quality AT services. "Flavor of the month" or "one-shot" training opportunities rarely lead to sustained changes in practice and other desired outcomes. This is especially true in potentially complex areas, such as collaborative work around the selection, acquisition, and—most importantly—effective use of AT by the students who require it. When planning for individual learning opportunities, teams may benefit from using the "Assistive Technology Professional Development and Training Planner" included at the end of this chapter. This and similar tools will help the planning team make a match between participants, content, levels of training, and learning outcomes.

Resources

The following resources support the content of this chapter.

Guide

- **Assistive Technology Trainer's Handbook** (*http://www.natenetwork.org/manuals-forms/at-trainers-handbook*)

    This guide, available online from NATE Network, provides professional development tips and strategies.

Training

- **AbleNet University** (*https://www.ablenetinc.com/resources/recorded_webinars*)

    AbleNet provides free live and recorded webinars on a broad range of topics, including recorded webinars specifically related to the Quality Indicators for Assistive Technology.

- **Assistive Technology Internet Modules (ATIM)** (*https://atinternetmodules.org*)

    The Ohio Center for Autism and Low Incidence (OCALI) and a consortium of partners have developed learning modules on a broad array of AT topics. These modules are available free of charge and can be used by individuals for self-study and by groups for collaborative learning.

- **ATIA Webinars** (*https://www.atia.org/webinars/*)

    The Assistive Technology Industry Association (ATIA) provides fee-based live and recorded webinars presented by experienced practitioners on a wide variety of AT topics.

- **Center on Technology and Disability** (*https://www.ctdinstitute.org/*)

    The Center on Technology and Disability work has been concluded, but the website—available through 2020—contains many free online learning opportunities, including a library of resources, webinars, and e-learning opportunities.

- **Closing the Gap** (*www.closingthegap.com*)

    Closing the Gap offers a variety of learning opportunities, including fee-based live and recorded webinars presented by experienced practitioners on a wide variety of AT topics.

- **National Center on Accessible Educational Materials at CAST** (*http://www.aem.cast.org*)

    The federally funded National Center on Accessible Educational Materials for Learning (AEM Center) offers a wide variety of webinars and online resources related to the procurement and provision of accessible materials and technologies.

- **Center on Inclusive Technology and Education Systems at CAST** (*http://cites.cast.org*)

    The federally funded Center on Inclusive Technology and Education Systems offers resources and technical assistance to assist school districts with developing and sustaining technology balanced ecosystems that includes Assistive Technology, Educational Technology and Information Technology.

- **Perkins School for the Blind** (*http://www.perkinselearning.org/videos/webinar/assistive-technology*)

    Perkins provides training webinars on AT products for individuals with vision loss.

- **Rehabilitation Engineering and Assistive Technology Society of North America** (*http://www.resna.org/professional-development*)

    RESNA offers a variety of professional development opportunities related to AT.

Assistive Technology Professional Development and Training Planner

Topic: _____ Date of Training: _____

School/Agency: _____ Planning Team Members: _____

Audience:	Describe Evidence of Need:
Purpose of Training:	Brief Overview of Content:

Level of Training:

❏ Awareness ❏ Application

❏ Knowledge ❏ Mastery

Focus of Training:

❏ Devices

❏ Services

Content Learning Objectives:

Format(s) for Training:

❏ Face-to-face ❏ Online learning module

❏ Ongoing class ❏ Blog or wiki

❏ Online workshop ❏ Podcast

❏ Online credit course ❏ Video training

❏ Webinar ❏ Community of Practice

Describe:

Formats for Follow-up:

❏ Coaching ❏ Social media

❏ Mentoring ❏ Professional Learning Community

❏ Email/phone support

Describe:

(continued)

Expected Results for Students:	
Evaluation Measures:	
Resources Needed: ❑ Training coordination ❑ Instructor ❑ Funding source ❑ Training site (face-to-face or electronic) ❑ Registration, enrollment ❑ Electronic communications	Describe:

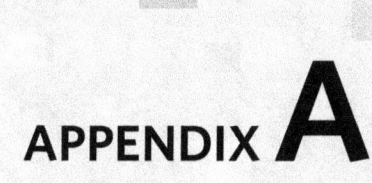

APPENDIX A

Quality Indicators for Assistive Technology Services, Intent Statements, and Common Errors

Quality Indicators for Consideration of Assistive Technology Needs

Consideration of the need for AT devices and services is an integral part of the educational process contained in IDEA for referral, evaluation, and IEP development. Although AT is considered at all stages of the process, the Consideration Quality Indicators are specific to the consideration of AT in the development of the IEP as mandated by the Individuals with Disabilities Education Act (IDEA). In most instances, the Quality Indicators are also appropriate for the consideration of AT for students who qualify for services under other legislation (e.g., 504, ADA).

1. **Assistive technology devices and services are *considered for all students with disabilities* regardless of type or severity of disability.**

    Intent: Consideration of assistive technology need is required by IDEA and is based on the unique educational needs of the student. Students are not excluded from consideration of AT for any reason (e.g., type of disability, age, administrative concerns).

2. **During the development of an individualized educational program, every IEP team consistently uses a *collaborative decision-making process* that supports systematic consideration of each student's possible need for assistive technology devices and services.**

    Intent: A collaborative process that ensures that all IEP teams effectively consider the assistive technology of students is defined, communicated, and consistently used throughout the agency. Processes may vary from agency to agency to most effectively address student needs under local conditions.

3. **IEP team members have the *collective knowledge and skills* needed to make informed assistive technology decisions and seek assistance when needed.**

    Intent: IEP team members combine their knowledge and skills to determine if assistive technology devices and services are needed to remove barriers to student performance. When the assistive technology needs are beyond the knowledge and scope of the IEP team, additional resources and support are sought.

4. **Decisions regarding the need for assistive technology devices and services are *based on the student's IEP goals and objectives, access to curricular and extracurricular activities, and progress in the general education curriculum.***

    Intent: As the IEP team determines the tasks the student needs to complete and develops the goals and objectives, the team considers whether assistive technology is required to accomplish those tasks.

5. **The IEP team *gathers and analyzes data* about the student, customary environments, educational goals, and tasks when considering a student's need for assistive technology devices and services.**

   Intent: The IEP team shares and discusses information about the student's present levels of achievement in relationship to the environments and tasks to determine if the student requires assistive technology devices and services to participate actively, work on expected tasks, and make progress toward mastery of educational goals.

6. **When assistive technology is needed, the IEP team *explores a range* of assistive technology devices, services, and other supports that address identified needs.**

   Intent: The IEP team considers various supports and services that address the educational needs of the student and may include no tech, low-tech, mid-tech, and/or high-tech solutions and devices. IEP team members do not limit their thinking to only those devices and services currently available within the district.

7. **The assistive technology consideration process and *results are documented in the IEP* and include a rationale for decisions and supporting evidence.**

   Intent: Even though IEP documentation may include a checkbox verifying that assistive technology has been considered, the reasons for the decisions and recommendations should be clearly stated. Supporting evidence may include the results of assistive technology assessments, data from device trials, differences in achievement with and without assistive technology, student preferences for competing devices, and teacher observations, among others.

Common Errors

1. AT is considered for students with severe disabilities only.

2. No one on the IEP team is knowledgeable regarding AT.

3. The team does not use a consistent process based on data about the student, environment, and tasks to make decisions.

4. Consideration of AT is limited to those items that are familiar to team members or are available in the district.

5. Team members fail to consider access to the curriculum and IEP goals in determining if the student requires AT to receive FAPE.

6. If the student does not need AT, team fails to document the basis of its decisions.

Quality Indicators for Assessment of Assistive Technology Needs

Applying the Quality Indicators for Assessment of Assistive Technology Needs is a process conducted by a team, used to identify tools and strategies to address a student's specific needs. The issues that lead to an AT assessment may be simple and quickly answered or more complex and challenging. Assessment takes place when these issues are beyond the scope of the problem solving that occurs as a part of normal service delivery.

1. *Procedures* **for all aspects of assistive technology assessment are clearly defined and consistently applied.**

   Intent: Throughout the educational agency, personnel are well informed and trained about assessment procedures and how to initiate them. There is consistency throughout the agency in the conducting of assistive technology assessments. Procedures may include—but are not limited to—initiating an assessment, planning and conducting an assessment, conducting trials, reporting results, and resolving conflicts.

2. **Assistive technology assessments are conducted by a team with the** *collective knowledge and skills needed* **to determine possible assistive technology solutions that address the needs and abilities of the student, demands of the customary environments, educational goals, and related activities.**

   Intent: Team membership is flexible and varies according to the knowledge and skills needed to address student needs. The student and family are active team members. Various team members bring different information and strengths to the assessment process.

3. **All assistive technology assessments include a functional assessment in the student's** *customary environments*, **such as the classroom, lunchroom, playground, home, community setting, or work place.**

   Intent: The assessment process includes activities that occur in the student's current or anticipated environments because characteristics and demands in each may vary. Team members work together to gather specific data and relevant information in identified environments to contribute to assessment decisions.

4. **Assistive technology assessments, including needed trials, are completed within** *reasonable timelines.*

   Intent: Assessments are initiated in a timely fashion and proceed according to a timeline the IEP team determines to be reasonable based on the complexity of student needs and assessment questions. Timelines comply with applicable state and agency requirements.

5. **Recommendations from assistive technology assessments are *based on data* about the student, environments, and tasks.**

   Intent: The assessment includes information about the student's needs and abilities, demands of various environments, educational tasks, and objectives. Data may be gathered from sources, such as student performance records, results of experimental trials, direct observation, interviews with students or significant others, and anecdotal records.

6. **The assessment provides the IEP team with clearly *documented recommendations* that guide decisions about the selection, acquisition, and use of assistive technology devices and services.**

   Intent: A written rationale is provided for any recommendations that are made. Recommendations may include assessment activities and results, suggested devices and alternative ways of addressing needs, services required by the student and others, and suggested strategies for implementation and use.

7. **Assistive technology needs are *reassessed* any time changes in the student, the environments, and/or the tasks result in the student's needs not being met with current devices and services.**

   Intent: An assistive technology assessment is available any time it is needed due to changes that have affected the student. The assessment can be requested by the parent or any other member of the IEP team.

Common Errors

1. Procedures for conducting AT assessment are not defined, or are not customized to meet the student's needs.

2. A team approach to assessment is not utilized.

3. Individuals participating in an assessment do not have the skills necessary to conduct the assessment, and do not seek additional help.

4. Team members don't have adequate time to conduct assessment processes, including necessary trials with AT.

5. Communication between team members is not clear.

6. The student is not involved in the assessment process.

7. When the assessment is conducted by any team other than the student's IEP team, the needs of the student or expectations for the assessment are not communicated.

Quality Indicators for Including Assistive Technology in the IEP

The Individuals with Disabilities Education Improvement Act (IDEA) requires that the IEP team consider AT needs in the development of every Individualized Education Program (IEP). Once the IEP team has reviewed assessment results and determined that AT is needed for provision of a free, appropriate, public education (FAPE), it's important that the IEP document reflects the team's determination as clearly as possible. The Quality Indicators for AT in the IEP help the team describe the role of AT in the child's educational program.

1. **The education agency has *guidelines for documenting* assistive technology needs in the IEP and requires their consistent application.**

    Intent: The education agency provides guidance to IEP teams about how to effectively document assistive technology needs, devices, and services as a part of specially designed instruction, related services, or supplementary aids and services.

2. **All *services* that the IEP team determines are needed to support the selection, acquisition, and use of assistive technology devices are designated in the IEP.**

    Intent: The provision of assistive technology services is critical to the effective use of assistive technology devices. It is important that the IEP describes the assistive technology services needed for student success. Such services may include evaluation, customization or maintenance of devices, coordination of services, and training for the student, family, and professionals, among others.

3. **The IEP illustrates that assistive technology is a *tool to support achievement of goals* and progress in the general curriculum by establishing a clear relationship between student needs, assistive technology devices and services, and the student's goals and objectives.**

    Intent: Most goals are developed before decisions about assistive technology are made. However, this does not preclude the development of additional goals, especially those related specifically to the appropriate use of assistive technology.

4. **IEP content regarding assistive technology use is written in language that describes how assistive technology contributes to achievement of *measurable and observable outcomes*.**

    Intent: Content that describes measurable and observable outcomes for assistive technology use enables the IEP team to review the student's progress and determine whether the assistive technology has had the expected impact on student participation and achievement.

5. **Assistive technology is included in the IEP in a manner that provides a *clear and complete description* of the devices and services to be provided and used to address student needs and achieve expected results.**

   Intent: IEPs are written so that participants in the IEP meeting and others who use the information to implement the student's program understand what technology is to be available, how it is to be used, and under what circumstances. Jargon should be avoided.

Common Errors

1. IEP teams do not know how to include AT in IEPs.
2. IEPs including AT use a formulaic approach to documentation. All IEPs are developed in a similar fashion and the unique needs of the child are not addressed.
3. AT is included in the IEP, but the relationship to goals and objectives is unclear.
4. AT devices are included in the IEP, but no AT services support the use.
5. AT expected results are not measurable or observable.

Quality Indicators for Assistive Technology Implementation

Assistive technology implementation pertains to the ways that assistive technology devices and services, as included in the IEP (including goals/objectives, related services, supplementary aids and services, and accommodations or modifications) are delivered and integrated into the student's educational program. Assistive technology implementation involves people working together to support the student using assistive technology to accomplish expected tasks necessary for active participation and progress in customary educational environments.

1. **Assistive technology implementation proceeds according to a *collaboratively developed plan*.**

   Intent: Following IEP development, all those involved in implementation work together to develop a written action plan that provides detailed information about how the AT will be used in specific educational settings, what will be done, and who will do it.

2. **Assistive technology is *integrated* into the curriculum and daily activities of the student across environments.**

   Intent: Assistive technology is used when and where it is needed to facilitate the student's access to, and mastery of, the curriculum. Assistive technology may facilitate active participation in educational activities, assessments, extracurricular activities, and typical routines.

3. **Persons supporting the student across all environments in which the assistive technology is expected to be used *share responsibility* for implementation of the plan.**

   Intent: All persons who work with the student know their roles and responsibilities, are able to support the student using assistive technology, and are expected to do so.

4. **Persons supporting the student provide opportunities for the student to use a *variety of strategies—including assistive technology* and to learn which strategies are most effective for particular circumstances and tasks.**

   Intent: When and where appropriate, students are encouraged to consider and use alternative strategies to remove barriers to participation or performance. Strategies may include the student's natural abilities, use of assistive technology, other supports, or modifications to the curriculum, task, or environment.

5. ***Learning opportunities* for the student, family, and staff are an integral part of implementation.**

   Intent: Learning opportunities needed by the student, staff, and family are based on how the assistive technology will be used in each unique environment. Training and technical assistance are planned and implemented as ongoing processes based on current and changing needs.

6. **Assistive technology implementation is initially based on assessment *data* and is adjusted based on performance data.**

   Intent: Formal and informal assessment data guide initial decision-making and planning for AT implementation. As the plan is carried out, student performance is monitored and implementation is adjusted in a timely manner to support student progress.

7. **Assistive technology implementation includes *management and maintenance of equipment* and materials.**

   Intent: For technology to be useful, it's important that equipment management responsibilities are clearly defined and assigned. Though specifics may differ based on the technology, some general areas may include organization of equipment and materials; responsibility for acquisition, set-up, repair, and replacement in a timely fashion; and assurance that equipment is operational.

Common Errors

1. Implementation is expected to be smooth and effective without addressing specific components in a plan. Team members assume that everyone understands what needs to happen and knows what to do.

2. Plans for implementation are created and carried out by one IEP team member.

3. The team focuses on device acquisition and does not discuss implementation.

4. An implementation plan is developed that is incompatible with the instructional environments.

5. No one takes responsibility for the care and maintenance of AT devices and so they are not available or in working order when needed.

6. Contingency plans for dealing with broken or lost devices are not made in advance.

Quality Indicators for Evaluation of the Effectiveness of Assistive Technology

This area addresses the evaluation of the effectiveness of the AT devices and services that are provided to individual students. It includes data collection, documentation, and analysis to monitor changes in student performance resulting from the implementation of assistive technology services. Student performance is reviewed in order to identify if, when, or where modifications and revisions to the implementation are needed.

1. **Team members share *clearly defined responsibilities* to ensure that data are collected, evaluated, and interpreted by capable and credible team members.**

    Intent: Each team member is accountable for ensuring that the data collection process determined by the team is implemented. Individual roles in the collection and review of the data are assigned by the team. Data collection, evaluation, and interpretation are led by persons with relevant training and knowledge. It can be appropriate for different individual team members to conduct these tasks.

2. **Data are collected on specific student achievement that has been identified by the team and is *related to one or more goals.***

    Intent: In order to evaluate the success of assistive technology use, data are collected on various aspects of student performance and achievement. Targets for data collection include the student's use of assistive technology to progress toward mastery of relevant IEP and curricular goals and to enhance participation in extracurricular activities at school and in other environments.

3. **Evaluation of effectiveness includes the *quantitative and qualitative measurement of changes* in the student's performance and achievement.**

    Intent: Changes targeted for data collection are observable and measurable so that data are as objective as possible. Changes identified by the IEP team for evaluation may include accomplishment of relevant tasks, how assistive technology is used, student preferences, productivity, participation, independence, quality of work, speed and accuracy of performance, and student satisfaction, among others.

4. **Effectiveness is evaluated *across environments* during naturally occurring and structured activities.**

   Intent: Relevant tasks within each environment where the assistive technology is to be used are identified. Data needed and procedures for collecting those data in each environment are determined.

5. **Data are collected to provide teams with a means for *analyzing student achievement and identifying supports and barriers* that influence assistive technology use to determine what changes, if any, are needed.**

   Intent: Teams regularly analyze data on multiple factors that may influence success or lead to errors in order to guide decision-making. Such factors include not only the student's understanding of expected tasks and ability to use assistive technology, but also student preferences, intervention strategies, training, and opportunities to gain proficiency.

6. ***Changes are made* in the student's assistive technology services and educational program when evaluation data indicate that such changes are needed to improve student achievement.**

   Intent: During the process of reviewing evaluation data, the team decides whether changes or modifications need to be made in the assistive technology, expected tasks, or factors within the environment. The team acts on those decisions and supports their implementation.

7. **Evaluation of effectiveness is a dynamic, responsive, *ongoing process* that is reviewed periodically.**

   Intent: Scheduled data collection occurs over time and changes in response to both expected and unexpected results. Data collection reflects measurement strategies appropriate to the individual student's needs. Team members evaluate and interpret data during periodic progress reviews.

Common Errors

1. An observable, measurable student behavior is not specified as a target for change.

2. Team members do not share responsibility for evaluation of effectiveness.

3. An environmentally appropriate means of data collection and strategies has not been identified.

4. A schedule of program review for possible modification is not determined before implementation begins.

Quality Indicators for Assistive Technology in Transition

Transition plans for students who use assistive technology address the ways the student's use of assistive technology devices and services are transferred from one setting to another. Assistive technology transition involves people from different classrooms, programs, buildings, or agencies working together to ensure continuity. Self-determination, advocacy, and implementation are critical issues for transition planning.

1. ***Transition plans address assistive technology needs*** **of the student, including roles and training needs of team members, subsequent steps in assistive technology use, and follow-up after transition takes place.**

    Intent: The comprehensive transition plan required by IDEA assists the receiving agency/team to successfully provide needed supports for the AT user. This involves assigning responsibilities and establishing accountability.

2. **Transition *planning empowers the student* using assistive technology *to participate* in the transition planning at a level appropriate to age and ability.**

    Intent: Specific self-determination skills are taught that enable the student to gradually assume responsibility for participation and leadership in AT transition planning as capacity develops. AT tools are provided, as needed, to support the student's participation.

3. ***Advocacy related to assistive technology use is recognized as critical*** **and planned for by the teams involved in transition.**

    Intent: Everyone involved in transition advocates for the student's progress, including the student's use of AT. Specific advocacy tasks related to AT use are addressed and may be carried out by the student, the family, staff members, or a representative.

4. ***AT requirements in the receiving environment*** **are identified during the transition planning process.**

    Intent: Environmental requirements, skill demands, and needed AT support are determined in order to plan appropriately. This determination is made collaboratively and with active participation by representatives from sending and receiving environments.

5. **Transition planning for students using assistive technology proceeds according to an *individualized timeline*.**

    Intent: Transition planning timelines are adjusted based on specific needs of the student and differences in environments. Timelines address well-mapped action steps with specific target dates and ongoing opportunities for reassessment.

6. **Transition plans address specific *equipment, training, and funding issues* such as transfer or acquisition of assistive technology, manuals, and support documents.**

    Intent: A plan is developed to ensure AT equipment, hardware, and software arrives in working condition accompanied by any needed manuals. Provisions for ongoing maintenance and technical support are included in the plan.

Common Errors

1. Lack of self-determination, self-awareness, and self-advocacy on the part of the individual with a disability (or advocate).

2. Lack of adequate long-range planning on the part of sending and receiving agencies (timelines).

3. Inadequate communication and coordination.

4. Failure to address funding responsibility.

5. Inadequate evaluation process (e.g., lack of documentation, insufficient data, poor communication).

6. Philosophical differences between sending and receiving agencies.

7. Lack of understanding of the law and of their responsibilities.

Quality Indicators for Administrative Support of Assistive Technology Services

This area defines the critical areas of administrative support and leadership for developing and delivering assistive technology services. It involves the development of policies, procedures, and other supports necessary to improve quality of services and sustain effective assistive technology programs.

1. **The education agency has *written procedural guidelines* that ensure equitable access to assistive technology devices and services for students with disabilities if required for a free, appropriate, public education (FAPE).**

    Intent: Clearly written procedural guidelines help ensure that students with disabilities have the assistive technology devices and services they require for educational participation and benefit. Access to assistive technology is ensured regardless of severity of disability, educational placement, geographic location, or economic status.

2. **The education agency *broadly disseminates* clearly defined procedures for accessing and providing assistive technology services and supports the implementation of those guidelines.**

    Intent: Procedures are readily available in multiple formats to families and school personnel in special and general education. All are aware of how to locate the procedures and are expected to follow procedures whenever appropriate.

3. **The education agency includes appropriate assistive technology responsibilities in *written descriptions of job requirements* for each position in which activities impact assistive technology services.**

    Intent: Appropriate responsibilities and the knowledge, skills, and actions required to fulfill them are specified for positions from the classroom through the central office. These descriptions will vary depending on the position and may be reflected in a position description, assignment of duty statement, or some other written description.

4. **The education agency employs *personnel with the competencies* needed to support quality assistive technology services within their primary areas of responsibility at all levels of the organization.**

    Intent: Although different knowledge, skills, and levels of understanding are required for various jobs, all understand and are able to fulfill their parts in developing and maintaining a collaborative system of effective assistive technology services to students.

5. **The education agency includes *assistive technology in the technology planning and budgeting process.***

    Intent: A comprehensive, collaboratively developed technology plan provides for the technology needs of all students in general education and special education.

6. **The education agency provides access to *ongoing learning opportunities about assistive technology* for staff, family, and students.**

    Intent: Learning opportunities are based on the needs of the student, the family, and the staff and are readily available to all. Training and technical assistance include any topic pertinent to the selection, acquisition, or use of assistive technology or any other aspect of assistive technology service delivery.

7. **The education agency uses a *systematic process to evaluate* all components of the agency-wide assistive technology program.**

    Intent: The components of the evaluation process include, but are not limited to, planning, budgeting, decision-making, delivering AT services to students, and evaluating the impact of AT services on student achievement. There are clear, systematic evaluation procedures that all administrators know about and use on a regular basis at central office and building levels.

Common Errors

1. If policies and guidelines are developed, they are not known widely enough to assure equitable application by all IEP teams.

2. It is not clearly understood that the primary purpose of AT in school settings is to support the implementation of the IEP for the provision of a free, appropriate, public education (FAPE).

3. Personnel have been appointed to head AT efforts, but resources to support those efforts have not been allocated (time, a budget for devices, professional development, etc.).

4. AT leadership personnel try or are expected to do all of the AT work and fail to meet expectations.

5. AT services are established but their effectiveness is never evaluated.

Quality Indicators for Professional Development and Training in Assistive Technology

This area defines the critical elements of quality professional development and training in assistive technology. Assistive technology professional development and training efforts should arise out of an ongoing, well-defined, sequential, and comprehensive plan. Such a plan can develop and maintain the abilities of individuals at all levels of the organization to participate in the creation and provision of quality AT services. The goal of assistive technology professional development and training is to increase educators' knowledge and skills in a variety of areas including, but not limited to these areas: collaborative processes; a continuum of tools, strategies, and services; resources; legal issues; action planning; and data collection and analysis. Audiences for professional development and training include students, parents or caregivers, special education teachers, educational assistants, support personnel, general education personnel, administrators, AT specialists, and others involved with students.

1. **Comprehensive assistive technology professional development and training** *support the understanding that assistive technology devices and services enable students to accomplish IEP goals and objectives and make progress in the general curriculum.*

    Intent: The Individuals with Disabilities Education Act (IDEA) requires the provision of a free, appropriate, public education (FAPE) for all children with disabilities. The Individualized Education Program (IEP) defines FAPE for each student. The use of AT enables students to participate in and benefit from FAPE. The focus of all AT professional development and training activities is to increase the student's ability to make progress in the general curriculum and accomplish IEP goals and objectives.

2. **The education agency has an assistive technology professional development and training** *plan that identifies the audiences, the purposes, the activities, the expected results, evaluation measures, and funding* **for assistive technology professional development and training.**

   Intent: The opportunity to learn the appropriate techniques and strategies is provided for each person involved in the delivery of assistive technology services. Professional development and training are offered at a variety of levels of expertise and are pertinent to individual roles.

3. **The content of comprehensive assistive technology professional development and training** *addresses all aspects of the selection, acquisition, and use* **of assistive technology.**

   Intent: AT professional development and training address the development of a wide range of assessment, collaboration, and implementation skills that enable educators to provide effective AT interventions for students. The AT professional development and training plan includes, but is not limited to collaborative processes; the continuum of tools, strategies, and services; resources; legal issues; action planning; and data collection.

4. **Assistive technology professional development and training address and are** *aligned with other local, state, and national professional development initiatives.*

   Intent: For many students with disabilities, assistive technology is required for active participation in local, state, and national educational initiatives. Content of the professional development and training includes information about how the use of assistive technology supports the participation of students with disabilities in these initiatives.

5. **Assistive technology professional development and training include** *ongoing learning opportunities that utilize local, regional, and national resources.*

   Intent: Professional development and training opportunities enable individuals to meet present needs and increase their knowledge of AT for use in the future. Training in AT occurs frequently enough to address new and emerging technologies and practices, and is available on a repetitive and continuous schedule. A variety of AT professional development and training resources are used.

6. **Professional development and training in assistive technology follow** *research-based models for adult learning* **that include multiple formats and are delivered at multiple skill levels.**

   Intent: The design of professional development and training for AT recognizes adults as diverse learners who bring various levels of prior knowledge and experience to the training, and can benefit from differentiated instruction using a variety of formats and diverse timeframes (e.g., workshops, distance learning, follow-up assistance, ongoing technical support).

7. **The effectiveness of assistive technology professional development and training is** *evaluated by measuring changes in practice that result in improved student performance.*

   Intent: Evidence is collected regarding the results of AT professional development and training. The professional development and training plan is modified based on these data in order to ensure changes to educational practice that result in improved student performance.

Common Errors

1. The educational agency does not have a comprehensive plan for ongoing AT professional development and training.

2. The educational agency's plan for professional development and training is not based on AT needs assessment and goals.

3. Outcomes for professional development are not clearly defined and effectiveness is not measured in terms of practice and student performance.

4. A continuum of ongoing professional development and training is not available.

5. Professional development and training focuses on the tools and not the process related to determining student needs and integrating technology into the curriculum.

6. Professional development and training is provided for special educators but not for administrators, general educators, and instructional technology staff.

APPENDIX B

Self-Evaluation Matrices for the Quality Indicators in Assistive Technology Services

Introduction to the QIAT Self-Evaluation Matrices

The Quality Indicators in Assistive Technology (QIAT) Self-Evaluation Matrices were developed in response to formative evaluation data indicating a need for a model that could assist in the application of the Quality Indicators for Assistive Technology Services in Schools (Zabala et al., 2000). The QIAT Matrices are based on the idea that change does not happen immediately, but rather moves toward the ideal in a series of steps that take place over time. The QIAT Matrices use the Innovation Configuration Matrix (ICM) developed by Hall and Hord (1985) as a structural model. The ICM provides descriptive steps ranging from the unacceptable to the ideal that can be used as benchmarks to determine the current status of practice related to a specific goal or objective, and guide continuous improvement toward the ideal. It enables users to determine areas of strength that can be built upon, as well as areas of challenge that need improvement.

When the QIAT Matrices are used to guide a collaborative self-assessment conducted by a diverse group of stakeholders within an agency, the information gained can be used to plan for changes that lead to improvement throughout the organization in manageable and attainable steps. The QIAT Matrices can also be used to evaluate the level to which expected or planned-for changes have taken place by periodically analyzing changes in service delivery over time.

When completed by an individual or team, the results of the self-assessment can be used to measure areas of strength and plan for needed professional development, training, or support for the individual or team. When an individual or team uses the QIAT Matrices, however, it is important to realize that the results can only reasonably reflect perceptions of the services in which that individual or team is involved and may not reflect the typical services within the organization. Since a primary goal of QIAT is to increase the quality and consistency of assistive technology (AT) services to *all* students throughout the organization, the perception that an individual or small group is working at the level of best practices does not necessarily mean that the need for quality and consistency of services has been met throughout the organization. The descriptive steps included in the QIAT Matrices are meant to provide illustrative examples and may not be specifically appropriate, as written, for all environments. People using the QIAT Matrices may wish to revise the descriptive steps to align them more closely for specific environments. However, when doing this, care must be taken that the revised steps do not compromise the intent of the quality indictor to which they apply.

The QIAT Matrices document is a companion document to the list of Quality Indicators and Intent Statements. The original six indicator areas were validated by research in 2004 and revisions were made in 2005, 2012, and 2015. For more information, please refer to the indicators and intent statements on the QIAT website at *www.qiat.org*. Before an item in the QIAT Matrices is discussed and rated, we recommend the groups read the entire item in the list of Quality Indicators and Intent Statements so that the intent of the item is clear.

References for QIAT Matrices

Hall, G. E. and Hord, S. M. (1987) *Change in Schools: Facilitating the Process.* Ithaca: State University of New York Press.

QIAT Community. (2015). Quality indicators for assistive technology services. Retrieved April 5, 2015 from *http://qiat.org/indicators.html*

Zabala, J. S. (2007). *Development and evaluation of quality indicators for assistive technology services.* University of Kentucky Doctoral Dissertations. Paper 517. Retrieved from *http://uknowledge.uky.edu/gradschool_diss/517*

Zabala, J. S., Bowser, G., Blunt, M., Carl, D. F., Davis, S., Deterding, C., Foss, T., Korsten, J., Hamman, T., Hartsell, K., Marfilius, S. W., McCloskey-Dale, S., Nettleton, S. D., & Reed, P. (2000). Quality indicators for assistive technology services. *Journal of Special Education Technology, 15*(4), 25-36.

Zabala, J. S., & Carl, D. F. (2005). Quality indicators for assistive technology services in schools. In D.L. Edyburn, K. Higgins, & R. Boone (Eds.), *The handbook of special education technology research and practice* (pp. 179-207). Whitefish Bay, WI: Knowledge by Design, Inc.

Quality Indicators for *Consideration* of Assistive Technology Needs

QUALITY INDICATOR	UNACCEPTABLE		
1. Assistive technology (AT) devices and services are *considered for all students with disabilities* regardless of type or severity of disability.	1 AT is not considered for students with disabilities.	2 AT is considered only for students with severe disabilities or students in specific disability categories.	
2. During the development of the individualized educational program (IEP), every IEP team consistently uses a *collaborative decision-making process* that supports systematic consideration of each student's possible need for AT devices and services.	1 No process is established for IEP teams to use to make AT decisions.	2 A process is established for IEP teams to use to make AT decisions but it is not collaborative.	
3. IEP team members have the *collective knowledge and skills* needed to make informed AT decisions and seek assistance when needed.	1 The team does not have the knowledge or skills needed to make informed AT decisions. The team does not seek help when needed.	2 Individual team members have some of the knowledge and skills needed to make informed AT decisions. The team does not seek help when needed.	
4. Decisions regarding the need for AT devices and services *are based on the student's IEP goals and objectives, access to curricular and extracurricular activities, and progress in the general education curriculum.*	1 Decisions about a student's need for AT are not connected to IEP goals or the general curriculum.	2 Decisions about a student's need for AT are based on either access to the curriculum/IEP goals or the general curriculum, not both.	
5. The IEP team *gathers and analyzes data* about the student, customary environments, educational goals, and tasks when considering a student's need for AT devices and services.	1 The IEP team does not gather and analyze data to consider a student's need for AT devices and services.	2 The IEP team gathers and analyzes data about the student, customary environments, educational goals, or tasks, but not all, when considering a student's need for AT devices and services.	
6. When AT is needed, the IEP team *explores a range* of AT devices, services, and other supports that address identified needs.	1 The IEP team does not explore a range of AT devices, services, and other supports to address identified needs.	2 The IEP team considers a limited set of AT devices, services, and other supports.	
7. The AT consideration process and *results are documented in the IEP* and include a rationale for the decision and supporting evidence.	1 The consideration process and results are not documented in the IEP.	2 The consideration process and results are documented in the IEP but do not include a rationale for the decision and supporting evidence.	

		PROMISING PRACTICES
3 AT is considered for all students with disabilities, but the consideration is inconsistently based on the unique educational needs of the student.	4 AT is considered for all students with disabilities and the consideration is generally based on the unique educational needs of the student.	5 AT is considered for all students with disabilities and the consideration is consistently based on the unique educational needs of the student.
3 A collaborative process is established but not generally used by IEP teams to make AT decisions.	4 A collaborative process is established and generally used by IEP teams to make AT decisions.	5 A collaborative process is established and consistently used by IEP teams to make AT decisions.
3 Team members sometimes combine knowledge and skills to make informed AT decisions. The team does not always seek help when needed.	4 Team members generally combine their knowledge and skills to make informed AT decisions. The team seeks help when needed.	5 The team consistently uses collective knowledge and skills to make informed AT decisions. The team seeks help when needed.
3 Decisions about a student's need for AT sometimes are based on both the student's IEP goals and general education curricular tasks.	4 Decisions about a student's need for AT generally are based on both the student's IEP goals and general education curricular tasks.	5 Decisions about a student's need for AT consistently are based on both the student's IEP goals and general education curricular tasks.
3 The IEP team sometimes gathers and analyzes data about the student, customary environments, educational goals, and tasks when considering a student's need for AT devices and services.	4 The IEP team generally gathers and analyzes data about the student, customary environments, educational goals, and tasks when considering a student's need for AT devices and services.	5 The IEP team consistently gathers and analyzes data about the student, customary environments, educational goals, and tasks when considering a student's need for AT devices and services.
3 The IEP team sometimes explores a range of AT devices, services, and other supports.	4 The IEP team generally explores a range of AT devices, services, and other supports.	5 The IEP team always explores a range of AT devices, services, and other supports to address identified needs.
3 The consideration process and results are documented in the IEP and sometimes include a rationale for the decision and supporting evidence.	4 The consideration process and results are documented in the IEP and generally include a rationale for the decision and supporting evidence.	5 The consideration process and results are documented in the IEP and consistently include a rationale for the decision and supporting evidence.

Quality Indicators for *Assessment* of Assistive Technology Needs

QUALITY INDICATOR	UNACCEPTABLE		
1. *Procedures* for all aspects of AT assessment are clearly defined and consistently applied.	1 No procedures are defined.	2 Some assessment procedures are defined, but not generally used.	
2. AT assessments are conducted by a *team with the collective knowledge and skills needed* to determine possible AT solutions that address the needs and abilities of the student, demands of the customary environments, educational goals, and related activities.	1 A designated individual with no prior knowledge of the student's needs or technology conducts assessments.	2 A designated person or group conducts assessments but lacks either knowledge of AT or of the student's needs, environments, or tasks.	
3. All AT assessments include a functional assessment in the student's *customary environments*, such as the classroom, lunchroom, playground, home, community setting, or work place.	1 No component of the AT assessment is conducted in any of the student's customary environments.	2 No component of the AT assessment is conducted in any of the customary environments; however, data about the customary environments are sought.	
4. AT assessments, including needed trials, are completed within *reasonable timelines*.	1 AT assessments are not completed within agency timelines.	2 AT assessments are frequently out of compliance with timelines.	
5. Recommendations from AT assessments are *based on data* about the student, environments, and tasks.	1 Recommendations are not data-based.	2 Recommendations are based on incomplete data from limited sources.	
6. The assessment provides the IEP team with clearly *documented recommendations* that guide decisions about the selection, acquisition, and use of AT devices and services.	1 Recommendations are not documented.	2 Documented recommendations include only devices. Recommendations about services are not documented.	
7. AT needs are *reassessed* anytime changes in the student, the environments, and/or the tasks result in the student's needs not being met with current devices or services.	1 AT needs are not reassessed.	2 AT needs are only reassessed when requested. Reassessment is done formally and no ongoing AT assessment takes place.	

		PROMISING PRACTICES
3 Procedures are defined and used only by specialized personnel.	4 Procedures are clearly defined and generally used in both special and general education.	5 Everyone involved in the assessment process uses clearly defined procedures.
3 A team conducts assessments with limited input from individuals who have knowledge of AT or of the student's needs, environments, and tasks.	4 A collaborative team whose members have direct knowledge of the student's needs, environments, and tasks, and knowledge of AT generally conducts assessments.	5 A collaborative, flexible team formed on the basis of knowledge of the individual student's needs, environments, and tasks, and expertise in AT consistently conducts assessments.
3 Functional components of AT assessments are sometimes conducted in the student's customary environments.	4 Functional components of AT assessments are generally conducted in the student's customary environments.	5 Functional components of AT assessments are consistently conducted in the student's customary environments.
3 AT assessments are completed within a reasonable timeline and may or may not include initial trials.	4 AT assessments are completed within a reasonable timeline and include at least initial trials.	5 AT assessments are conducted in a timely manner and include a plan for ongoing assessment and trials in customary environments.
3 Recommendations are sometimes based on data about student performance on typical tasks in customary environments.	4 Recommendations are generally based on data about student performance on typical tasks in customary environments.	5 Recommendations are consistently based on data about student performance on typical tasks in customary environments.
3 Documented recommendations may or may not include sufficient information about devices and services to guide decision-making and program development.	4 Documented recommendations generally include sufficient information about devices and services to guide decision-making and program development.	5 Documented recommendations consistently include sufficient information about devices and services to guide decision-making and program development.
3 AT needs are reassessed on an annual basis or upon request. Reassessment may include some ongoing and formal assessment strategies.	4 AT use is frequently monitored. AT needs are generally reassessed if current tools and strategies are ineffective. Reassessment generally includes ongoing assessment strategies and includes formal assessment, if indicated.	5 AT use is frequently monitored. AT needs are consistently reassessed if current tools and strategies are ineffective. Reassessment generally includes ongoing assessment strategies and includes formal assessment, if indicated.

Quality Indicators for Including Assistive Technology in the IEP

QUALITY INDICATOR	UNACCEPTABLE		
1. The education agency has *guidelines for documenting* **AT needs in the IEP and requires their consistent application.**	1 The agency does not have guidelines for documenting AT in the IEP.	2 The agency has guidelines for documenting AT in the IEP but team members are not aware of them.	
2. All *services* **that the IEP team determines are needed to support the selection, acquisition, and use of AT devices are designated in the IEP.**	1 AT devices and services are not documented in the IEP.	2 Some AT devices and services are minimally documented. Documentation does not include sufficient information to support effective implementation.	
3. The IEP illustrates that AT is a *tool to support achievement of goals* **and progress in the general curriculum by establishing a clear relationship between the student's needs, AT devices and services, and the student's goals and objectives.**	1 AT use is not linked to IEP goals and objectives or participation and progress in the general curriculum.	2 AT use is sometimes linked to IEP goals and objectives but not linked to the general curriculum.	
4. IEP content regarding AT use is written in language that describes how AT contributes to achievement of *measurable and observable outcomes.*	1 The IEP does not describe outcomes to be achieved through AT use.	2 The IEP describes outcomes to be achieved through AT use, but they are not measurable.	
5. AT is included in the IEP in a manner that provides a *clear and complete* **description of the devices and services to be provided and is used to address student needs and achieve expected results.**	1 Devices and services needed to support AT use are not documented.	2 Some devices and services are documented but they do not adequately support AT use.	

		PROMISING PRACTICES
3 The agency has guidelines for documenting AT in the IEP and members of some teams are aware of them.	4 The agency has guidelines for documenting AT in the IEP and members of most teams are aware of them.	5 The agency has guidelines for documenting AT in the IEP and members of all teams are aware of them.
3 Required AT devices and services are documented. Documentation sometimes includes sufficient information to support effective implementation.	4 Required AT devices and services are documented. Documentation generally includes sufficient information to support effective implementation.	5 Required AT devices and services are documented. Documentation consistently includes sufficient information to support effective implementation.
3 AT use is linked to IEP goals and objectives and sometimes linked to the general curriculum.	4 AT use is linked to IEP goals and objectives and is generally linked to the general curriculum.	5 AT use is linked to the IEP goals and objectives and is consistently linked to the general curriculum.
3 The IEP describes outcomes to be achieved through AT use, but only some are measurable.	4 The IEP generally describes observable, measurable outcomes to be achieved through AT use.	5 The IEP consistently describes observable, measurable outcomes to be achieved through AT use.
3 Devices and services are documented and are sometimes adequate to support AT use.	4 Devices and services are documented and are generally adequate to support AT use.	5 Devices and services are documented and are consistently adequate to support AT use.

Quality Indicators for Assistive Technology *Implementation*

QUALITY INDICATOR	UNACCEPTABLE		
1. AT implementation proceeds according to a *collaboratively developed plan*.	1 There is no implementation plan.	2 Individual team members may develop AT implementation plans independently.	
2. AT is *integrated* into the curriculum and daily activities of the student across environments.	1 AT included in the IEP is rarely used.	2 AT is used in isolation with no links to the student's curriculum and/or daily activities.	
3. Persons supporting the student across all environments in which the AT is expected to be used *share responsibility* for implementation of the plan.	1 Responsibility for implementation is not accepted by any team member.	2 Responsibility for implementation is assigned to one team member.	
4. Persons supporting the student provide opportunities for the student to use *a variety of strategies*—including AT—and to learn which strategies are most effective for particular circumstances and tasks.	1 No strategies are provided to support the accomplishment of tasks.	2 Only one strategy is provided to support the accomplishment of tasks.	
5. *Learning opportunities* for the student, family, and staff are an integral part of implementation.	1 AT needs for learning opportunities have not been determined.	2 AT learning opportunity needs are initially identified for student, family, and staff, but no training has been provided.	
6. AT implementation is initially based on assessment *data* and is adjusted based on performance data.	1 AT implementation is based on equipment availability and limited knowledge of team members, not on student data.	2 AT implementation is loosely based on initial assessment data and rarely adjusted.	
7. AT implementation includes management and maintenance of equipment and materials.	1 Equipment and materials are not managed or maintained. Students rarely have access to the equipment and materials they require.	2 Equipment and materials are managed and maintained on a crisis basis. Students frequently do not have access to the equipment and materials they require.	

		PROMISING PRACTICES
3 Some team members collaborate in the development of an AT implementation plan.	4 Most team members collaborate in the development of AT implementation plan.	5 All team members collaborate in the development of a comprehensive AT implementation plan.
3 AT is sometimes integrated into the student's curriculum and daily activities.	4 AT is generally integrated into the student's curriculum and daily activities.	5 AT is fully integrated into the student's curriculum and daily activities.
3 Responsibility for implementation is shared by some team members in some environments.	4 Responsibility for implementation is generally shared by most team members in most environments.	5 Responsibility for implementation is consistently shared among team members across all environments.
3 Multiple strategies are provided. Students are sometimes encouraged to select and use the most appropriate strategy for each task.	4 Multiple strategies are provided. Students are generally encouraged to select and use the most appropriate strategy for each task.	5 Multiple strategies are provided. Students are consistently encouraged to select and use the most appropriate strategy for each task.
3 Initial AT learning opportunities are sometimes provided to student, family, and staff.	4 Initial and follow-up AT learning opportunities are generally provided to student, family, and staff	5 Ongoing AT learning opportunities are provided to student, family, and staff as needed, based on changing needs.
3 AT implementation is based on initial assessment data and is sometimes adjusted as needed based on student progress.	4 AT implementation is based on initial assessment data and is generally adjusted as needed based on student progress.	5 AT implementation is based on initial assessment data and is consistently adjusted as needed based on student progress.
3 Equipment and materials are managed and maintained so that students sometimes have access to the equipment and materials they require.	4 Equipment and materials are managed and maintained so that students generally have access to the equipment and materials they require.	5 Equipment and materials are effectively managed and maintained so that students consistently have access to the equipment and materials they require.

Quality Indicators for *Evaluation of the Effectiveness* of Assistive Technology

QUALITY INDICATOR	UNACCEPTABLE		
1. Team members share *clearly defined responsibilities* to ensure that data are collected, evaluated, and interpreted by capable and credible team members.	1 Responsibilities for data collection, evaluation, or interpretation are not defined.	2 Responsibilities for data collection, evaluation, or interpretation of data are assigned to one team member.	
2. Data are collected on specific student achievement that has been identified by the team and is *related to one or more goals*.	1 Team neither identifies specific changes in student behaviors expected from AT use nor collects data.	2 Team identifies student behaviors and collects data, but the behaviors are either not specific or not related to IEP goals.	
3. Evaluation of effectiveness includes the *quantitative and qualitative* measurement of changes in the student's performance and achievement.	1 Effectiveness is not evaluated.	2 Evaluation of effectiveness is based not on student performance, but rather on subjective opinion.	
4. Effectiveness is evaluated *across environments* including during naturally occurring opportunities as well as structured activities.	1 Effectiveness is not evaluated in any environment.	2 Effectiveness is evaluated only during structured opportunities in controlled environments (e.g., massed trials data).	
5. Data are collected so teams can analyze *student achievement and identify supports and barriers* that influence AT use and determine what changes, if any, are needed.	1 No data are collected or analyzed.	2 Data are collected but are not analyzed.	
6. *Changes are made* in the student's AT services and educational program when evaluation data indicate that such changes are needed to improve student achievement.	1 Program changes are never made.	2 Program changes are made in the absence of data.	
7. Evaluation of effectiveness is a dynamic, responsive, *ongoing process* that is reviewed periodically.	1 No process is used to evaluate effectiveness.	2 Evaluation of effectiveness only takes place annually, but the team does not make program changes based on data.	

		PROMISING PRACTICES
3 Responsibilities for collection, evaluation, and interpretation of data are shared by some team members.	4 Responsibilities for collection, evaluation, and interpretation of data are shared by most team members.	5 Responsibilities for collection, evaluation, and interpretation of data are consistently shared by team members.
3 Team identifies specific student behaviors related to IEP goals, but inconsistently collects data.	4 Team identifies specific student behaviors related to IEP goals, and generally collects data.	5 Team identifies specific student behaviors related to IEP goals, and consistently collects data on changes in those behaviors.
3 Evaluation of effectiveness is not consistent or is based on limited data about student performance.	4 Evaluation of effectiveness is generally based on quantitative and qualitative data about student performance from a few sources.	5 Effectiveness is consistently evaluated using both quantitative and qualitative data about student's performance obtained from a variety of sources.
3 Effectiveness is evaluated during structured activities across environments and a few naturally occurring opportunities.	4 Effectiveness is generally evaluated during naturally occurring opportunities and structured activities in multiple environments.	5 Effectiveness is consistently evaluated during naturally occurring opportunities and structured activities in multiple environments.
3 Data are superficially analyzed.	4 Data are sufficiently analyzed most of the time.	5 Data are sufficiently analyzed all of the time.
3 Program changes are loosely linked to student performance data.	4 Program changes are generally linked to student performance data.	5 Program changes are consistently linked to student performance data.
3 Evaluation of effectiveness only takes place annually and the team uses the data to make annual program changes	4 Evaluation of effectiveness takes place on an on-going basis and team generally uses the data to make program changes.	5 Evaluation of effectiveness takes place on an on-going basis and the team consistently uses the data to make program changes.

Quality Indicators for Assistive Technology in *Transition*

QUALITY INDICATOR	UNACCEPTABLE	
1. *Transition plans address the AT needs of the student,* including roles and training needs of team members, subsequent steps in AT use, and follow-up after transition takes place.	1 Transition plans do not address AT needs.	2 Transition plans rarely address AT needs, critical roles, steps, or follow-up.
2. Transition *planning empowers the student* using AT to participate in the transition planning at a level appropriate to age and ability.	1 Student is not present.	2 Student may be present but does not participate or input is ignored.
3. *Advocacy related to AT use is recognized as critical* and planned for by the teams involved in transition.	1 No one advocates for AT use or the development of student self-determination skills.	2 Advocacy rarely occurs for AT use or the development of student self-determination skills.
4. *AT requirements in the receiving environment* are identified during the transition planning process.	1 AT requirements in the receiving environment are not identified.	2 AT requirements in the receiving environment are rarely identified.
5. Transition planning for students using AT proceeds according to an *individualized timeline*.	1 Individualized timelines are not developed to support transition planning for students using AT.	2 Individualized timelines are developed, but do not support transition planning for students using AT.
6. Transition plans address specific *equipment, training, and funding* issues, such as transfer or acquisition of AT, manuals, and support documents.	1 The plans do not address AT equipment, training, and funding issues.	2 The plans rarely address AT equipment, training, and/or funding issues.

		PROMISING PRACTICES
3 Transition plans sometimes address AT needs but may not include critical roles, steps, or follow-up.	4 Transition plans always address AT needs and usually include critical roles, steps, or follow-up.	5 Transition plans consistently address AT needs and all team members are involved and knowledgeable about critical roles, steps, and follow-up.
3 Student sometimes participates and some student input is considered.	4 Student participates and student input is generally reflected in the transition plan.	5 Student is a full participant and student input is consistently reflected in the transition plan.
3 Advocacy sometimes occurs for AT use and the development of student self-determination skills.	4 Advocacy usually occurs for AT use and the development of student self-determination skills.	5 Advocacy consistently occurs for AT use and the development of student self-determination skills.
3 AT requirements in the receiving environment are identified, some participants are involved, and some requirements are addressed.	4 AT requirements in the receiving environment are identified, most participants are involved, and most requirements are addressed.	5 AT requirements in the receiving environment are consistently identified by all participants.
3 Individualized timelines are sometimes developed and support transition planning for students using AT.	4 Individualized timelines are generally developed and support transition planning for students using AT.	5 Individualized timelines are consistently developed and support transition planning for students using AT.
3 The plans sometimes address AT equipment, training, or funding issues.	4 The plans usually address AT equipment, training, and funding issues.	5 The plans consistently address AT equipment, training, and funding issues.

Quality Indicators for *Administrative Support* of Assistive Technology

QUALITY INDICATOR	UNACCEPTABLE		
1. The education agency has *written procedural guidelines* that ensure equitable access to AT devices and services for students with disabilities, if required for a free appropriate public education (FAPE).	1 No written procedural guidelines are in place.	2 Written procedural guidelines for few components of AT service delivery (e.g., assessment or consideration) are in place.	
2. The education agency *broadly disseminates* clearly defined procedures for accessing and providing AT services, and supports the implementation of those guidelines.	1 No procedures disseminated and no plan to disseminate.	2 A plan for dissemination exists, but has not been implemented.	
3. The education agency includes appropriate AT responsibilities in *written descriptions of job requirements* for each position in which activities impact AT services.	1 No job requirements relating to AT are written.	2 Job requirements related to AT are written only for a few specific personnel who provide AT services.	
4. The education agency employs *personnel with the competencies* needed to support quality AT services within their primary areas of responsibility at all levels of the organization.	1 AT competencies are not considered in hiring, assigning, or evaluating personnel.	2 AT competencies are recognized as an added value in an employee but are not sought.	
5. The education agency includes *AT in the technology planning and budgeting process.*	1 There is no planning and budgeting process for AT.	2 AT planning and budgeting is a special education function that is not included in the agency-wide technology planning and budgeting process.	
6. The education agency provides access to *ongoing learning opportunities about AT for staff, family, and students.*	1 No learning opportunities related to AT are provided.	2 Learning opportunities related to AT are provided on a crisis-basis only. Learning opportunities may not be available to all who need them.	
7. The education agency uses a *systematic process to evaluate* all components of the agency-wide AT program.	1 The agency-wide AT program is not evaluated.	2 Varying procedures are used to evaluate some components of the agency-wide AT program.	

			PROMISING PRACTICES
	3 Written procedural guidelines that address several components of AT service delivery are in place.	4 Written procedural guidelines that address most components of AT service delivery are in place.	5 Comprehensive written procedural guidelines that address all components of AT service delivery are in place.
	3 Procedures are disseminated to a few staff who work directly with AT.	4 Procedures are disseminated to most agency personnel and generally used.	5 Procedures are disseminated to all agency personnel and consistently used.
	3 Job requirements related to AT are written for most personnel who provide AT services but are not clearly aligned to job responsibilities.	4 Job requirements related to AT are written for most personnel who provide AT services and are generally aligned to job responsibilities.	5 Job requirements related to AT are written for all personnel who provide AT services and are clearly aligned to job responsibilities.
	3 AT competencies are recognized and sought for specific personnel.	4 AT competencies are generally valued and used in hiring, assigning, and evaluating personnel.	5 AT competencies are consistently valued and used in hiring, assigning, and evaluating personnel.
	3 AT is sometimes included in the agency-wide technology planning and budgeting process, but in a way that is inadequate to meet AT needs throughout the agency.	4 AT is generally included in agency-wide technology planning and budgeting process in a way that meets most AT needs throughout the agency.	5 AT is included in the agency-wide technology planning and budgeting process in a way that meets AT needs throughout the agency.
	3 Learning opportunities related to AT are provided to some individuals on a pre-defined schedule.	4 Learning opportunities related to AT are provided on a pre-defined schedule to most individuals with some follow-up opportunities.	5 Learning opportunities related to AT are provided on an ongoing basis to address the changing needs of students with disabilities, their families, and the staff who serve them.
	3 A systematic procedure is inconsistently used to evaluate a few components of the agency-wide AT program.	4 A systematic procedure is generally used to evaluate most components of the agency-wide AT program.	5 A systematic procedure is consistently used throughout the agency to evaluate all components of the agency-wide AT program.

Quality Indicators for *Professional Development and Training* in Assistive Technology

QUALITY INDICATOR	UNACCEPTABLE		
1. Comprehensive AT professional development and training *support the understanding that AT devices and services enable students to accomplish IEP goals and objectives and make progress in the general curriculum.*	1 There is no professional development and training in the use of AT.	2 Professional development and training address only technical aspects of AT tools and/or are not related to use for academic achievement.	
2. The education agency has an AT professional development and training plan that *identifies the audiences, purposes, activities, expected results, evaluation measures, and funding* for AT professional development and training.	1 There is no plan for AT professional development and training.	2 The plan includes unrelated activities done on a sporadic basis for a limited audience.	
3. The content of comprehensive AT professional development and training *addresses all aspects of the selection, acquisition, and use* of AT.	1 There is no professional development and training related to selection, acquisition, and use of AT.	2 Professional development and training address few aspects of selection, acquisition, and use of AT.	
4. AT professional development and training address and are *aligned with other local, state, and national professional development initiatives.*	1 Professional development and training do not consider other initiatives.	2 Professional development and training rarely align with other initiatives.	
5. AT professional development and training include ongoing learning opportunities that utilize local, regional, and/or national resources.	1 There are no professional development and training opportunities.	2 Professional development and training occur infrequently.	
6. Professional development and training in AT follow *research-based models for adult learning* that include multiple formats and are delivered at multiple skill levels.	1 Professional development and training never consider adult learning.	2 Professional development and training rarely consider models for adult learning strategies.	
7. The effectiveness of AT professional development and training is *evaluated by measuring changes* in practice that result in improved student performance.	1 Changes in practice are not measured.	2 Changes in practice are rarely measured.	

		PROMISING PRACTICES
3 Some professional development and training include strategies for use of AT devices and services to facilitate academic achievement.	4 Most professional development and training include strategies for use of AT devices and services to facilitate academic achievement.	5 All professional development and training include strategies for use of AT devices and services to facilitate academic achievement.
3 The plan includes some elements (e.g., variety of activities, purpose, levels) for some audiences.	4 The plan includes most elements of a comprehensive plan for most audiences.	5 The comprehensive AT professional development plan encompasses all elements, audiences, and levels.
3 Professional development and training address some aspects of selection, acquisition, and use of AT.	4 Professional development and training address most aspects of selection, acquisition, and use of AT.	5 Professional development and training address all aspects of selection, acquisition, and use of AT.
3 Professional development and training sometimes align with other initiatives.	4 Professional development and training generally align with other initiatives.	5 Professional development and training consistently align with other initiatives as appropriate.
3 Professional development and training are sometimes provided.	4 Professional development and training are generally provided.	5 Professional development and training opportunities are provided on a comprehensive, repetitive, and continuous schedule, utilizing appropriate local, regional, and national resources.
3 Professional development and training sometimes consider research-based adult learning strategies.	4 Professional development and training generally consider research-based adult learning strategies.	5 Professional development and training consistently consider research-based adult learning strategies.
3 Changes in practice are measured using a variety of measures but may not be related to student performance.	4 Changes in practice are usually measured using a variety of reliable measures linked to improved student performance.	5 Changes in practice are consistently measured using a variety of reliable measures linked to improved student performance.

APPENDIX C

Self-Evaluation Matrices Worksheets

QIAT Matrix Worksheet for *Consideration* of AT Needs

After completing the matrix:

- Record the self-rating numbers on this summary sheet.
- Circle the variation number to the right of each indicator.
- Connect the circles to create a depiction of strengths and areas of concern.
- Analyze strengths and challenges in each area.
- Prioritize action items that will lead to improvement.

CONSIDERATIONS OF AT NEEDS	RATING #
1. Assistive technology devices and services are considered for all students with disabilities regardless of type or severity of disability.	1 2 3 4 5
2. During the development of the individualized educational program, every IEP team consistently uses a collaborative decision-making process that supports systematic consideration of each student's possible need for assistive technology devices and services.	1 2 3 4 5
3. IEP team members have the collective knowledge and skills needed to make informed assistive technology decisions and seek assistance when needed.	1 2 3 4 5
4. Decisions regarding the need for assistive technology devices and services are based on the student's IEP goals and objectives, access to curricular and extracurricular activities, and progress in the general education curriculum.	1 2 3 4 5
5. The IEP team gathers and analyzes data about the student, customary environments, educational goals, and tasks when considering a student's need for assistive technology devices and services.	1 2 3 4 5
6. When assistive technology is needed, the IEP team explores a range of assistive technology devices, services, and other supports that address identified needs.	1 2 3 4 5
7. The assistive technology consideration process and results are documented in the IEP and include a rationale for the decision and supporting evidence.	1 2 3 4 5

STRENGTHS IN THIS AREA:

GREATEST CHALLENGES IN THIS AREA:

ACTIONS NEEDED TO LOWER BARRIERS TO IMPROVEMENT (List, then prioritize):

QIAT Matrix Worksheet for *Assessment* of AT Needs

After completing the matrix:

- Record the self-rating numbers on this summary sheet.
- Circle the variation number to the right of each indicator.
- Connect the circles to create a depiction of strengths and areas of concern.
- Analyze strengths and challenges in each area.
- Prioritize action items that will lead to improvement.

ASSESSMENT OF AT NEEDS	RATING #
1. Procedures for all aspects of assistive technology assessment are clearly defined and consistently applied.	1　2　3　4　5
2. Assistive technology assessments are conducted by a team with the collective knowledge and skills needed to determine possible assistive technology solutions that address the needs and abilities of the student, demands of the customary environments, educational goals, and related activities.	1　2　3　4　5
3. All assistive technology assessments include a functional assessment in the student's customary environments, such as the classroom, lunchroom, playground, home, community setting, or work place.	1　2　3　4　5
4. Assistive technology assessments, including needed trials, are completed within reasonable timelines.	1　2　3　4　5
5. Recommendations from assistive technology assessments are based on data about the student, environments, and tasks.	1　2　3　4　5
6. The assessment provides the IEP team with clearly documented recommendations that guide decisions about the selection, acquisition, and use of assistive technology devices and services.	1　2　3　4　5
7. Assistive technology needs are reassessed any time changes in the student, the environments and/or the tasks result in the student's needs not being met with current devices and/or services.	1　2　3　4　5

STRENGTHS IN THIS AREA:

GREATEST CHALLENGES IN THIS AREA:

ACTIONS NEEDED TO LOWER BARRIERS TO IMPROVEMENT (List, then prioritize):

QIAT Matrix Worksheet for *Including AT in the IEP*

After completing the matrix:

- Record the self-rating numbers on this summary sheet.
- Circle the variation number to the right of each indicator.
- Connect the circles to create a depiction of strengths and areas of concern.
- Analyze strengths and challenges in each area.
- Prioritize action items that will lead to improvement.

INCLUDING AT IN THE IEP	RATING #
1. The education agency has guidelines for documenting assistive technology needs in the IEP and requires their consistent application.	1 2 3 4 5
2. All services that the IEP team determines are needed to support the selection, acquisition, and use of assistive technology devices are designated in the IEP.	1 2 3 4 5
3. The IEP illustrates that assistive technology is a tool to support achievement of goals and progress in the general curriculum by establishing a clear relationship between student needs, assistive technology devices and services, and the student's goals and objectives.	1 2 3 4 5
4. IEP content regarding assistive technology use is written in language that describes how assistive technology contributes to achievement of measurable and observable outcomes.	1 2 3 4 5
5. Assistive technology is included in the IEP in a manner that provides a clear and complete description of the devices and services to be provided and used to address student needs and achieve expected results.	1 2 3 4 5

STRENGTHS IN THIS AREA:

GREATEST CHALLENGES IN THIS AREA:

ACTIONS NEEDED TO LOWER BARRIERS TO IMPROVEMENT (List, then prioritize):

QIAT Matrix Worksheet for *AT Implementation*

After completing the matrix:

- Record the self-rating numbers on this summary sheet.
- Circle the variation number to the right of each indicator.
- Connect the circles to create a depiction of strengths and areas of concern.
- Analyze strengths and challenges in each area.
- Prioritize action items that will lead to improvement.

AT IMPLEMENTATION	RATING #
1. Assistive technology implementation proceeds according to a collaboratively developed plan.	1 2 3 4 5
2. Assistive technology is integrated into the curriculum and daily activities of the student across environments.	1 2 3 4 5
3. Persons supporting the student across all environments in which the assistive technology is expected to be used share responsibility for implementation of the plan.	1 2 3 4 5
4. Persons supporting the student provide opportunities for the student to use a variety of strategies–including assistive technology–and to learn which strategies are most effective for particular circumstances and tasks.	1 2 3 4 5
5. Learning opportunities for the student, family and staff are an integral part of implementation.	1 2 3 4 5
6. Assistive technology implementation is initially based on assessment data and is adjusted based on performance data.	1 2 3 4 5
7. Assistive technology implementation includes management and maintenance of equipment and materials.	1 2 3 4 5

STRENGTHS IN THIS AREA:

GREATEST CHALLENGES IN THIS AREA:

ACTIONS NEEDED TO LOWER BARRIERS TO IMPROVEMENT (List, then prioritize):

QIAT Matrix Worksheet for *Evaluation of Effectiveness* of AT

After completing the matrix:

- Record the self-rating numbers on this summary sheet.
- Circle the variation number to the right of each indicator.
- Connect the circles to create a depiction of strengths and areas of concern.
- Analyze strengths and challenges in each area.
- Prioritize action items that will lead to improvement.

EVALUATION OF EFFECTIVENESS	RATING #				
1. Team members share clearly defined responsibilities to ensure that data are collected, evaluated, and interpreted by capable and credible team members.	1	2	3	4	5
2. Data are collected on specific student achievement that has been identified by the team and is related to one or more goals.	1	2	3	4	5
3. Evaluation of effectiveness includes the quantitative and qualitative measurement of changes in the student's performance and achievement.	1	2	3	4	5
4. Effectiveness is evaluated across environments during naturally occurring opportunities as well as structured activities.	1	2	3	4	5
5. Data are collected to provide teams with a means for analyzing student achievement and identifying supports and barriers that influence assistive technology use to determine what changes, if any, are needed.	1	2	3	4	5
6. Changes are made in the student's assistive technology services and educational program when evaluation data indicate that such changes are needed for improved student achievement.	1	2	3	4	5
7. Evaluation of effectiveness is a dynamic, responsive, ongoing process that is reviewed periodically.	1	2	3	4	5

STRENGTHS IN THIS AREA:

GREATEST CHALLENGES IN THIS AREA:

ACTIONS NEEDED TO LOWER BARRIERS TO IMPROVEMENT (List, then prioritize):

QIAT Matrix Worksheet for *Assistive Technology Transition*

After completing the matrix:

- Record the self-rating numbers on this summary sheet.
- Circle the variation number to the right of each indicator.
- Connect the circles to create a depiction of strengths and areas of concern.
- Analyze strengths and challenges in each area.
- Prioritize action items that will lead to improvement.

AT TRANSITION	RATING #
1. Transition plans address the assistive technology needs of the student, including roles and training needs of team members, subsequent steps in assistive technology use, and follow-up after transition takes place.	1 2 3 4 5
2. Transition planning empowers the student using assistive technology to participate in the transition planning at a level appropriate to age and ability.	1 2 3 4 5
3. Advocacy related to assistive technology use is recognized as critical and planned for by the teams involved in transition.	1 2 3 4 5
4. AT requirements in the receiving environment are identified during the transition planning process.	1 2 3 4 5
5. Transition planning for students using assistive technology proceeds according to an individualized timeline.	1 2 3 4 5
6. Transition plans address specific equipment, training, and funding issues such as transfer or acquisition of assistive technology, manuals, and support documents.	1 2 3 4 5

STRENGTHS IN THIS AREA:

GREATEST CHALLENGES IN THIS AREA:

ACTIONS NEEDED TO LOWER BARRIERS TO IMPROVEMENT (List, then prioritize):

QIAT Worksheet for *Administrative Support* of AT Services

After completing the matrix:

- Record the self-rating numbers on this summary sheet.
- Circle the variation number to the right of each indicator.
- Connect the circles to create a depiction of strengths and areas of concern.
- Analyze strengths and challenges in each area.
- Prioritize action items that will lead to improvement.

ADMINISTRATIVE SUPPORT	RATING #				
1. The education agency has written procedural guidelines that ensure equitable access to assistive technology devices and services for students with disabilities, if required for a free and appropriate public education (FAPE).	1	2	3	4	5
2. The education agency broadly disseminates clearly defined procedures for accessing and providing assistive technology services and supports the implementation of those guidelines.	1	2	3	4	5
3. The education agency includes appropriate assistive technology responsibilities in written descriptions of job requirements for each position in which activities impact assistive technology services.	1	2	3	4	5
4. The education agency employs personnel with the competencies needed to support quality assistive technology services within their primary areas of responsibility at all levels of the organization.	1	2	3	4	5
5. The education agency includes assistive technology in the technology planning and budgeting process.	1	2	3	4	5
6. The education agency provides access to ongoing learning opportunities about assistive technology for staff, family, and students.	1	2	3	4	5
7. The education agency uses a systematic process to evaluate all components of the agency-wide assistive technology program.	1	2	3	4	5

STRENGTHS IN THIS AREA:

GREATEST CHALLENGES IN THIS AREA:

ACTIONS NEEDED TO LOWER BARRIERS TO IMPROVEMENT (List, then prioritize):

QIAT Worksheet for *Professional Development and Training* in AT

After completing the matrix:

- Record the self-rating numbers on this summary sheet.
- Circle the variation number to the right of each indicator.
- Connect the circles to create a depiction of strengths and areas of concern.
- Analyze strengths and challenges in each area.
- Prioritize action items that will lead to improvement.

PROFESSIONAL DEVELOPMENT AND TRAINING	RATING #
1. Comprehensive assistive technology professional development and training support the understanding that assistive technology devices and services enable students to accomplish IEP goals and objectives and make progress in the general curriculum.	1 2 3 4 5
2. The education agency has an AT professional development and training plan that identifies the audiences, the purposes, the activities, the expected results, evaluation measures, and funding for assistive technology professional development and training.	1 2 3 4 5
3. The content of comprehensive AT professional development and training addresses all aspects of the selection, acquisition, and use of assistive technology.	1 2 3 4 5
4. AT professional development and training address and are aligned with other local, state, and national professional development initiatives.	1 2 3 4 5
5. Assistive technology professional development and training include ongoing learning opportunities that utilize local, regional, and/or national resources.	1 2 3 4 5
6. Professional Development and Training in assistive technology follow research-based models for adult learning that include multiple formats and are delivered at multiple skill levels.	1 2 3 4 5
7. The effectiveness of assistive technology professional development and training is evaluated by measuring changes in practice that result in improved student performance.	1 2 3 4 5

STRENGTHS IN THIS AREA:

GREATEST CHALLENGES IN THIS AREA:

ACTIONS NEEDED TO LOWER BARRIERS TO IMPROVEMENT (List, then prioritize):

APPENDIX D

Legal References Related to Assistive Technology

Individuals with Disabilities Education Improvement Act of 2004 (IDEA 2004)

Public Law 108-446 and Title 34 of the Code of Federal Regulations

34 C.F.R. § 300.5 Assistive technology device

Assistive technology device means any item, piece of equipment, or product system, whether acquired commercially off the shelf, modified, or customized, that is used to increase, maintain, or improve the functional capabilities of a child with a disability. The term does not include a medical device that is surgically implanted, or the replacement of that device.

(Authority 20 U.S.C. 1401(1))

34 C.F.R. § 300.6 Assistive technology service

Assistive technology service means any service that directly assists a child with a disability in the selection, acquisition, or use of an assistive technology device. The term includes:

(a) The evaluation of the needs of a child with a disability, including a functional evaluation of the child in the child's customary environment;

(b) Purchasing, leasing, or otherwise providing for the acquisition of assistive technology devices by children with disabilities;

(c) Selecting, designing, fitting, customizing, adapting, applying, maintaining, repairing, or replacing assistive technology devices;

(d) Coordinating and using other therapies, interventions, or services with assistive technology devices, such as those associated with existing education and rehabilitation plans and programs;

(e) Training or technical assistance for a child with a disability or, if appropriate, that child's family; and

(f) Training or technical assistance for professionals (including individuals providing education or rehabilitation services), employers, or other individuals who provide services to, employ, or are otherwise substantially involved in the major life functions of that child.
(Authority: 20 U.S.C. 1401(2))

34 C.F.R. § 300.14 Equipment

Equipment means—

(b) All other items necessary for the functioning of a particular facility as a facility for the provision of educational services, including items such as instructional equipment and necessary furniture; printed, published and audio-visual instructional materials; telecommunications, sensory, and other technological aids and devices; and books, periodicals, documents, and other related materials.
(Authority: 20 U.S.C. 1401(7))

34 C.F.R. § 300.34 Related services

(a) General. Related services means transportation and such developmental, corrective, and other supportive services as are required to assist a child with a disability to benefit from special education, and includes speech-language pathology and audiology services, interpreting services, psychological services, physical and occupational therapy, recreation, including therapeutic recreation, early identification and assessment of disabilities in children, counseling services, including rehabilitation counseling, orientation and mobility services, and medical services for diagnostic or evaluation purposes. Related services also include school health services and school nurse services, social work services in schools, and parent counseling and training.

(b) Exception; services that apply to children with surgically implanted devices, including cochlear implants.

(1) Related services do not include a medical device that is surgically implanted, the optimization of that device's functioning (e.g., mapping), maintenance of that device, or the replacement of that device.

(2) Nothing in paragraph (b) (1) of this section—

(i) Limits the right of a child with a surgically implanted device (e.g., cochlear implant) to receive related services (as listed in paragraph (a) of this section) that are determined by the IEP Team to be necessary for the child to receive FAPE.

(ii) Limits the responsibility of a public agency to appropriately monitor and maintain medical devices that are needed to maintain the health and safety of the child, including breathing, nutrition, or operation of other bodily functions, while the child is transported to and from school or is at school; or

(iii) Prevents the routine checking of an external component of a surgically implanted device to make sure it is functioning properly, as required in § 300.113(b).

(Authority: 20 U.S.C. 1401(26))

34 C.F.R. § 300.39 Special education

(a) General.

(1) Special education means specially designed instruction, at no cost to the parents, to meet the unique needs of a child with a disability, including—

(b) Individual special education terms defined. The terms in this definition are defined as follows:

(3) Specially designed instruction means adapting, as appropriate to the needs of an eligible child under this part, the content, methodology, or delivery of instruction—

(i) To address the unique needs of the child that result from the child's disability; and

(ii) To ensure access of the child to the general curriculum, so that the child can meet the educational standards within the jurisdiction of the public agency that apply to all children.

(Authority: 20 U.S.C. 1401(29))

34 C.F.R. § 300.42 Supplementary aids and services

Supplementary aids and services means aids, services, and other supports that are provided in regular education classes, other education-related settings, and in extracurricular and nonacademic settings, to enable children with disabilities to be educated with nondisabled children to the maximum extent appropriate in accordance with §§ 300.114 through 300.116.

(Authority: 20 U.S.C. 1401(33))

34 C.F.R. §300.43 Transition services

(A) Transition services means a coordinated set of activities for a child with a disability that—

Is designed to be within a results-oriented process, that is focused on improving the academic and functional achievement of the child with a disability to facilitate the child's movement from school to post-school activities, including postsecondary education, vocational education, integrated employment (including supported employment), continuing and adult education, adult services, independent living, or community participation;

Is based on the individual child's needs, taking into account the child's strengths, preferences, and interests; and includes—

(i) Instruction;

(ii) Related services;

(iii) Community experiences;

(iv) The development of employment and other post-school adult living objectives; and

(v) If appropriate, acquisition of daily living skills and provision of a functional vocational evaluation.

(B) Transition services for children with disabilities may be special education, if provided as specially designed instruction, or a related service, if required to assist a child with a disability to benefit from special education.
(Authority 20 U.S.C. 1401(34))

34 C.F.R. § 300.44 Universal design

Universal design has the meaning given the term in section 3 of the Assistive Technology Act of 1998, as amended, 29 U.S.C. 3002.
(Authority: 20 U.S.C. 1401(35))

34 C.F.R § 300.105 Assistive technology

(a) Each public agency must ensure that assistive technology devices or assistive technology services, or both, as those terms are defined in §§ 300.5 and 300.6, respectively, are made available to a child with a disability if required as a part of the child's—

(1) Special education under § 300.36;

(2) Related services under § 300.34; or

(3) Supplementary aids and services under §§ 300.38 and 300.114(a)(2)(ii).

(b) On a case-by-case basis, the use of school-purchased assistive technology devices in a child's home or in other settings is required if the child's IEP Team determines that the child needs access to those devices in order to receive FAPE.
(Authority: 20 U.S.C. 1412(a)(1), 1412 (a)(12)(B)(i))

34 C.F.R. § 300.113 Routine checking of hearing aids and external components of surgically implanted medical devices.

(a) Hearing aids. Each public agency must ensure that hearing aids worn in school by children with hearing impairments, including deafness, are functioning properly.

(b) External components of surgically implanted medical devices.

(1) Subject to paragraph (b)(2) of this section, each public agency must ensure that the external components of surgically implanted medical devices are functioning properly.

(2) For a child with a surgically implanted medical device who is receiving special education and related services under this part, a public agency is not responsible for the post-surgical maintenance, programming, or replacement

of the medical device that has been surgically implanted (or of an external component of the surgically implanted medical device).

(Authority: 20 U.S.C. 1401(1), 1401(26)(B))

34 C.F.R. § 300.172 Access to instructional materials

(a) General. The State must—

(1) Adopt the National Instructional Materials Accessibility Standard (NIMAS), published as appendix C to part 300, for the purposes of providing instructional materials to blind persons or other persons with print disabilities, in a timely manner after publication of the NIMAS in the Federal Register on July 19, 2006 (71 FR 41084); and

(2) Establish a State definition of "timely manner" for purposes of paragraphs (b)(2) and (b)(3) of this section if the State is not coordinating with the National Instructional Materials Access Center (NIMAC) or (b)(3) and (c)(2) of this section if the State is coordinating with the NIMAC.

(b) Rights and responsibilities of SEA.

(1) Nothing in this section shall be construed to require any SEA to coordinate with the NIMAC.

(2) If an SEA chooses not to coordinate with the NIMAC, the SEA must provide an assurance to the Secretary that it will provide instructional materials to blind persons or other persons with print disabilities in a timely manner.

(3) Nothing in this section relieves an SEA of its responsibility to ensure that children with disabilities who need instructional materials in accessible formats, but are not included under the definition of blind or other persons with print disabilities in § 300.172(e)(1)(i) or who need materials that cannot be produced from NIMAS files, receive those instructional materials in a timely manner.

(4) In order to meet its responsibility under paragraphs (b)(2), (b)(3), and (c) of this section to ensure that children with disabilities who need instructional materials in accessible formats are provided those materials in a timely manner, the SEA must ensure that all public agencies take all reasonable steps to provide instructional materials in accessible formats to children with disabilities who need those instructional materials at the same time as other children receive instructional materials.

(c) Preparation and delivery of files. If an SEA chooses to coordinate with the NIMAC, as of December 3, 2006, the SEA must—

(1) As part of any print instructional materials adoption process, procurement contract, or other practice or instrument used for purchase of print instructional materials, must enter into a written contract with the publisher of the print instructional materials to—

(i) Require the publisher to prepare and, on or before delivery of the print instructional materials, provide to NIMAC electronic files containing the contents of the print instructional materials using the NIMAS, or

(ii) Purchase instructional materials from the publisher that are produced in, or may be rendered in, specialized formats.

(2) Provide instructional materials to blind persons or other persons with print disabilities in a timely manner.

(d) Assistive technology. In carrying out this section, the SEA, to the maximum extent possible, must work collaboratively with the State agency responsible for assistive technology programs.

(e) Definitions.

(1) In this section and § 300.210—

(i) 'Blind persons or other persons with print disabilities' means children served under this part who may qualify to receive books and other publications produced in specialized formats in accordance with the Act entitled "An Act to provide books for adult blind," approved March 3, 1931, 2 U.S.C 135a;

(ii) 'National Instructional Materials Access Center' or NIMAC means the center established pursuant to section 674(e) of the Act;

(iii) 'National Instructional Materials Accessibility Standard' or NIMAS has the meaning given the term in section 674(e)(3)(B) of the Act;

(iv) 'Specialized formats' has the meaning given the term in section 674(e)(3)(D) of the Act.

(2) The definitions in paragraph (e)(1) of this section apply to each State and LEA, whether or not the State or LEA chooses to coordinate with the NIMAC.
(Authority: 20 U.S.C. 1412(a)(23), 1474(e))

34 C.F.R. § 300.210 Purchase of instructional materials.

(a) General. Not later than December 3, 2006, an LEA that chooses to coordinate with the National Instructional Materials Access Center (NIMAC), when purchasing print instructional materials, must acquire those instructional materials in the same manner, and subject to the same conditions as an SEA under § 300.172.

(b) Rights of LEA.

(1) Nothing in this section shall be construed to require an LEA to coordinate with the NIMAC.

(2) If an LEA chooses not to coordinate with the NIMAC, the LEA must provide an assurance to the SEA that the LEA will provide instructional materials to blind persons or other persons with print disabilities in a timely manner.

(3) Nothing in this section relieves an LEA of its responsibility to ensure that children with disabilities who need instructional materials in accessible formats but are not included under the definition of blind or other persons with print disabilities in § 300.172(e)(1)(i) or who need materials that cannot be produced from NIMAS files, receive those instructional materials in a timely manner.
(Authority: 20 U.S.C. 1413(a)(6))

34 C.F.R. §300.320 Definition of Individualized Education Program

(a) General. As used in this part, the term individualized education program or IEP means a written statement of each child with a disability that is developed, reviewed, and revised in a meeting in accordance with §§300.320 through 300.324, and that must include—

(4) a statement of the special education and related services and supplementary aids and services, based on peer-reviewed research to the extent practicable, to be provided to the child, or on behalf of the child, and a statement of the program modifications or supports for school personnel that will be provided to enable the child—

(b) Transition services. Beginning not later than the first IEP to be in effect when the child turns 16, or younger if determined appropriate by the IEP Team, and updated annually, thereafter, the IEP must include—

(1) Appropriate measurable postsecondary goals based upon age appropriate transition assessments related to training, education, employment, and, where appropriate, independent living skills; and

(2) The transition services (including courses of study) needed to assist the child in reaching those goals.
(Authority: 20 U.S.C. 1414(d)(1)(A(i)(IV) and 1414(d)(1)(A)(i)(VIII))

34 C.F.R. § 300.324 Development, review, and revision of IEP

(a) Development of IEP—

(2) Consideration of special factors. The IEP team must—

(i) In the case of a child whose behavior impedes the child's learning or that of others, consider the use of positive behavioral interventions and supports, and other strategies, to address that behavior;

(ii) In the case of a child with limited English proficiency, consider the language needs of the child as those needs relate to the child's IEP;

(iii) In the case of a child who is blind or visually impaired, provide for instruction in Braille and the use of Braille unless the IEP Team determines, after an evaluation of the child's reading and writing skills, needs, and appropriate reading and writing media (including an evaluation of the child's future needs for instruction in Braille or the use of

Braille), that instruction in Braille or the use of Braille is not appropriate for the child;

(iv) Consider the communication needs of the child, and in the case of a child who is deaf or hard of hearing, consider the child's language and communication needs, opportunities for direct communications with peers and professional personnel in the child's language and communication mode, academic level, and full range of needs, including opportunities for direct instruction in the child's language and communication mode; and

(v) Consider whether the child needs assistive technology devices and services.

(Authority: 20 U.S.C. 1414 (d)(3)(B))

[Emphasis added]

34 C.F.R. § 300.704 State-level activities

(b) Other State-level activities

(4) Funds reserved under paragraph (b)(1) of this section also may be used to carry out the following activities:

(iv) To improve the use of technology in the classroom by children with disabilities to enhance learning;

(v) To support the use of technology, including technology with universal design principles and assistive technology devices, to maximize accessibility to the general education curriculum for children with disabilities;

(Authority: 20 U.S.C. 1411(e))

Appendix C to Part 300—National Instructional Materials Accessibility Standard (NIMAS)

Under sections 612(a)(23)(A) and 674(e)(4) of the Individuals with Disabilities Education Act, as amended by the Individuals with Disabilities Education Improvement Act of 2004, the Secretary of Education establishes the NIMAS. Under section 674(e)(4) of the Act, the NIMAS applies to print instructional materials published after July 19, 2006. The purpose of the NIMAS is to help increase the availability and timely delivery of print instructional materials in accessible formats to blind or other persons with print disabilities in elementary and secondary schools.

(See Appendix C to Part 300 for Technical Specifications—The Baseline Element Set)

Definitions from Other Statutes Referred to in IDEA 2004

An Act to Provide Books for the Adult Blind (March 3, 1931, 2 U.S.C. 135a) and Title 36 of the Code of Federal Regulations

36 C.F.R. § 701.10 Loans of library materials for blind and other physically handicapped persons.

(a) Program. In connection with the Library's program of service under the act of March 3, 1931 (46 Stat. 1487), as amended, its National Library Service for the Blind and Physically Handicapped provides books in raised characters (Braille), on sound reproduction recordings, or in any other form, under regulations established by the Librarian of Congress. The National Library Service also provides and maintains reproducers for such sound reproduction recordings for the use of blind and other physically handicapped residents of the United States, including the several States, Territories, Insular Possessions, and the District of Columbia, and American citizens temporarily domiciled abroad.

(b) Eligibility Criteria.

(1) following persons are eligible for such service:

(i) Blind persons whose visual acuity, as determined by competent authority, is 20/200 or less in the better eye with correcting glasses, or whose widest diameter if visual field subtends an angular distance no greater than 20 degrees.

(ii) Persons whose visual disability, with correction and regardless of optical measurement, is certified by competent authority as preventing the reading of standard printed material.

(iii) Persons certified by competent authority as unable to read or unable to use standard printed material as a result of physical limitations.

(iv) Persons certified by competent authority as having a reading disability resulting from organic dysfunction and of sufficient severity to prevent their reading printed material in a normal manner.

[39 Federal Register 20203, June 7, 1974, as amended at 46 Federal Register 48661, Oct. 2, 1981]

Legislative Branch Appropriations Act, Public Law 104-197

1996 Chafee Amendment to the Copyright Law

AN ACT

Making appropriations for the Legislative Branch for the fiscal year ending September 30, 1997, and for other purposes.

Be it enacted by the Senate and House of Representatives of the United States of America in Congress assembled, That the following sums are appropriated, out of any money in the Treasury not otherwise appropriated, for the Legislative Branch for the fiscal year ending September 30, 1997, and for other purposes, namely:

SEC. 316. Limitation on Exclusive Copyrights for Literary Works in Specialized Format for the Blind and Disabled. —

(a) In General—Chapter 1 of title 17, United States Code, is amended by adding after section 120 the following new section:

SEC.121. Limitations on exclusive rights: reproduction for blind or other people with disabilities

(a) Notwithstanding the provisions of sections 106 and 710, it is not an infringement of copyright for an authorized entity to reproduce or to distribute copies or phonorecords of a previously published, nondramatic literary work if such copies or phonorecords are reproduced or distributed in specialized formats exclusively for use by blind or other persons with disabilities.

(b)(1) Copies or phonorecords to which this section applies shall—

(A) not be reproduced or distributed in a format other than a specialized format exclusively for use by blind or other persons with disabilities;

(B) bear a notice that any further reproduction or distribution in a format other than a specialized format is an infringement; and

(C) include a copyright notice identifying the copyright owner and the date of the original publication.

(2) The provisions of this subsection shall not apply to standardized, secure, or norm-referenced tests and related testing material, or to computer programs, except the portions thereof that are in conventional human language (including descriptions of pictorial works) and displayed to users in the ordinary course of using the computer programs.

(c) For purposes of this section, the term—

(1) "authorized entity" means a nonprofit organization or a governmental agency that has a primary mission to provide specialized services relating to training, education, or adaptive reading or information access needs of blind or other persons with disabilities;

(2) "blind or other persons with disabilities" means individuals who are eligible or who may qualify in accordance with the Act entitled 'An Act to provide books for the adult blind', approved March 3, 1931 (2 U.S.C. 135a; 46 Stat. 1487) to receive books and other publications produced in specialized formats; and

(3) "specialized formats" means braille, audio, or digital text which is exclusively for use by blind or other persons with disabilities.

(d) Technical and Conforming Amendment—The table of sections for chapter 1 of title 17, United States Code, is amended by adding after the item relating to section 120 the following:

121. Limitations on exclusive rights: reproduction for blind or other people with disabilities.

Assistive Technology Act of 1998, Public Law 105-394

Section 3 Definitions and Rule

(a) DEFINITIONS—In this act...

(17) UNIVERSAL DESIGN—The term `universal design' means a concept or philosophy for designing and delivering products and services that are usable by people with the widest possible range of functional capabilities, which include products and services that are directly usable (without requiring assistive technologies) and products and services that are made usable with assistive technologies.

About the Authors

The QIAT Leadership Team

Gayl Bowser

Gayl Bowser, M.S. in Education, currently works as an independent consultant and is an adjunct faculty member at the University of Wyoming. Her work focuses on the creation of service systems that encourage the integration of technology into educational programs for students with disabilities. Formerly the coordinator of the Oregon Technology Access Program (OTAP) and the State of Oregon's specialist in assistive technology, Gayl currently provides assistive technology consultation, training, and technical assistance throughout the United States and internationally. Gayl has co-authored numerous publications about assistive technology services including *Education Tech Points: A Framework for Assistive Technology* and *Assistive Technology Pointers for Parents.*

Diana Foster Carl

Diana Foster Carl has a B.A. and M.A. in Psychology and is a Licensed Specialist in School Psychology in Texas. She has more than 35 years of experience in various capacities in public education, including leadership roles in national, state, and regional organizations. Currently, Diana works with CAST as part of its National Center on Accessible Educational Materials for Learning (the AEM Center). Diana is a former director of special education services at Region 4 Education Service Center in Houston, Texas, where she was lead facilitator of the Texas Assistive Technology Network for 12 years. Diana's daughter has cerebral palsy and uses a power wheelchair for mobility.

Terry Vernon Foss

Terry Vernon Foss has an M.Ed. with an emphasis in Special Education. Terry has been a special educator for more than 35 years in classrooms for students with autism and with severe and profound disabilities including speech, intellectual, and motor impairments. For the last 20+ years, she has been an assistive technology specialist for the Shawnee Mission School District in Kansas. Terry is a coauthor of *Every Move Counts* and *Every Move Counts Clicks and Chats.*

Kelly S. Fonner

Kelly Fonner has a B.S. in Special Education and an M.S. in Educational Technology with an emphasis in Rehabilitation/Special Education Technology. She has done continuing education in Adult Education and Special Education Technology. Kelly has been a teacher, para-educator, instructional media specialist, and assistive technology specialist. She is currently self-employed as a consultant in assistive and educational technology. She has worked for a statewide AT project and has been an instructor in university courses on AT. Since 1986 she has presented to schools, conferences, and families in 46 states and internationally on a wide range of topics in AT. Kelly is also the daughter of a person with an acquired physical disability, the sister-in-law of a woman with cerebral palsy, and the cousin of individuals with a teenager with Aspergers.

Jane Edgar Korsten

Jane Edgar Korsten holds a B.S. in Elementary Education and an M.A. in Speech Pathology and Audiology. She currently works as an independent consultant, a speech pathologist, and AT resource for individuals of all ages. She has worked in public schools, supported settings for adults, and had a private practice developing alternate communication systems for individuals who are non-verbal. She was the principal investigator on an Innovative Research Grant funded through the National Institutes of Health which led to the development of Every Move Counts, a sensory based approach to communication. Jane is a coauthor of *Every Move Counts, Every Move Counts Clicks and Chats,* and *How Do You Know It? How Do You Show It?*

Kathleen M. Lalk

Kathleen M. Lalk has a B.S. in Recreation Therapy and an M.S. in Educational Technology. For more than 20 years, she has served as an assistive technology specialist for Special School District in St. Louis County, Missouri. Her work includes support of students with disabilities, their families, and their educational team in the consideration, implementation, and evaluation of the use of assistive technology. She is also a consumer support provider for Missouri Assistive Technology.

Joan Breslin Larson

Joan Breslin Larso, an independent consultant, holds an M.Ed. in Adult Education. For years, Joan was the supervisor for low incidence disabilities and special education workforce at the Minnesota Department of Education. She has also consulted to other state organizations and schools on systems issues in AT. Joan has family members with disabilities, including a child who had an IEP and others with acquired disabilities.

Scott Marfilius

Scott Marfilius has an M.A. in Education (Curriculum and Instruction). Scott has worked with individuals with disabilities for more than 38 years, and for the past 34 years has been involved in implementing assistive technology services at various levels. Scott assists teams and individuals in assessing students' AT needs. Scott also works with universities and has assisted in reorganizing postsecondary curriculum to infuse technology throughout the teacher-preparation experience. He also consults with individuals and businesses to determine adaptations that are needed in workplace settings. Scott's focus areas in assistive technology include computer access and technologies that assist those with cognitive and learning disabilities.

Susan R. McCloskey

Susan R. McCloskey, MS, CCC-SLP, is a speech language pathologist who worked for the PA Assistive Technology Center/PaTTAN in Pennsylvania and is now chairperson of the Volusia Adaptive Assistive Technology Team (VAATT) in Daytona Beach, FL. She is a past steering committee member for ASHA's Division 12: Augmentative and Alternative Communication. Susan has consulted nationwide with teams whose focus has been to integrate assistive technology into the classroom. She has been a trainer of environmental communication teaching (ECT) since 1989. She is currently involved in implementing the SCERTS project, focused on students on the autism spectrum in her district and lives in Ponce Inlet, FL.

Penny R. Reed

Penny R. Reed has an M.S. and Ph.D. in Special Education and a B.S. in Elementary Education. Dr. Reed has been a teacher, consultant, and administrator in the field of special education and assistive technology. She regularly provides consultation and training on a variety of topics related to assistive technology assessment and service delivery with a special focus on helping school districts improve their delivery of assistive technology services. She is the author and coauthor of numerous publications about assistive technology services, including *Education Tech Points: A Framework for Assistive Technology*.

Joy Smiley Zabala

Joy Smiley Zabala, Ed.D., holds degrees in Elementary and Early Childhood Education and Special Education Personnel Preparation. Currently she is the Director of Technical Assistance for CAST. Joy is an experienced general and special educator who has worked for more than 30 years with educators, families, and students across the US and abroad to expand the use of assistive and accessible technologies, accessible materials, and Universal Design for Learning for the participation and achievement of all learners across the lifespan. Dr. Zabala is the developer of the SETT Framework, a past president of the Technology and Media Division of the Council for Exceptional Children, and serves as a faculty member for the Center on Technology and Disability.

www.ingramcontent.com/pod-product-compliance
Lightning Source LLC
Chambersburg PA
CBHW081748100526
44592CB00015B/2345